TRIUMPH
B O O K S

ODD MAN IN

ODD MAN IN

HOCKEY'S EMERGENCY GOALIES AND THE WILDEST ONE-DAY JOB IN SPORTS

STEPHEN WHYNO

TRIUMPH
BOOKS

No part of this publication may be reproduced, stored in a retrieval system, or transmitted in any form by any means, electronic, mechanical, photocopying, or otherwise, without the prior written permission of the publisher, Triumph Books LLC, 814 North Franklin Street, Chicago, Illinois 60610.

Library of Congress Cataloging-in-Publication Data available upon request.

This book is available in quantity at special discounts for your group or organization. For further information, contact:

Triumph Books LLC
814 North Franklin Street
Chicago, Illinois 60610
(312) 337-0747
www.triumphbooks.com

Printed in U.S.A.
ISBN: 978-1-62937-999-9
Design by Nord Compo

To my parents,
who fostered my love of hockey and put up
with it when it became my professional life.
Thank you for everything.

CONTENTS

FOREWORD

I WAS SITTING in my hotel room in Washington, D.C., when the nearly unthinkable happened.

Both of Carolina's goaltenders were injured during their game in Toronto, so the Hurricanes had to turn to an emergency backup goaltender. Great.

I would have loved it if a minor leaguer would have been around to get the chance in the NHL he's been waiting for, but that's not how it worked. Zamboni driver David Ayres walked out of the tunnel.

David was 42—my age at the time—and he was stepping between the pipes for a contender in the middle of a playoff race. I was preparing for my game the next day between the Penguins and Capitals.

Rod Brind'Amour, a teammate of mine for a brief time during my rookie year in Philadelphia, coaches Carolina, and I couldn't imagine what he was thinking at the time. (Editor's note: more on that later.)

I thought it was a train wreck waiting to happen. The Maple Leafs had Auston Matthews, Mitch Marner, and one of the best offenses in hockey. Ayres was a practice goalie who had never played professional hockey.

What did Ayres do? Well, after allowing goals on the first two shots, he was perfect. Eight more saves, a win, and his moment in the spotlight.

It was must-see TV.

It always is when an "EBUG" goes into a game. It never seemed to ever happen, and now it has happened twice in a meaningful way since 2017. Yeah, that was when accountant Scott Foster stopped all seven shots he faced to win a game for Chicago.

Maybe the speed of the game is the reason. Concussion spotters are watching and can pull any player off the ice.

Coaches always tell players to crash the net. What happens then? Speaking from experience, goalies get hurt.

When injuries piled up in Florida a few years ago, old Robb Tallas, the Panthers' goalie coach, was ready to strap on the pads until Roberto Luongo saved the day by returning from the hospital. That night set the stage for Ayres and Foster to put their names in hockey history.

I had my own EBUG experience back in 2010, the year we dressed seven goalies with the Flyers as the injury bug jumped around. The team called up a kid who recently finished his college career to back me up on a Sunday afternoon.

When we were comfortably up by a few goals late in the game, I asked one of the assistant coaches if they wanted to get the kid in. How would he ever get that chance again?

Turns out the kid was Carter Hutton, who signed an NHL contract with San Jose that summer. He has played 10 seasons.

Nobody could have seen that coming, but that's what makes every EBUG situation a must-watch. The equipment manager, financial advisor, or vending machine repairman who is next to get the call won't know it's coming either—until someone comes up to them to tell them to get in the net.

Hopefully one day the NHL will figure out how to keep an extra pro goalie around who might be able to show what he can do after years of toiling in the minors. Until then, the next EBUG could be just about anybody.

—Brian Boucher

November 11, 2021

Brian Boucher played 371 games over 13 NHL seasons for the Philadelphia Flyers, Phoenix Coyotes, San Jose Sharks, Calgary Flames, Chicago Blackhawks, Columbus Blue Jackets, and Carolina Hurricanes. In 2003–04 with the Coyotes, he set the record for the longest shutout streak in the modern era at 332:01 and in 2010 helped the Flyers reach the Stanley Cup Final. He is currently an ESPN analyst.

INTRODUCTION
What's an Emergency Backup Goaltender?

S ITTING AT THE SAME PLACE he celebrated the day after his life changed, Scott Foster still can't come to grips with it.

"It doesn't really make sense," he said. "None of it makes sense."

Foster isn't just talking about his own experience in the spotlight, playing 14 unforgettable minutes in a National Hockey League game for the Chicago Blackhawks in 2018. He means the entire concept of an emergency backup goaltender, also known as an EBUG.

It's not possible in any other sport and nearly impossible to replicate in any other walk of life. If a football team runs out of quarterbacks, there isn't someone waiting nearby who used to play the position. Someone else on the roster has to do it. If a baseball team runs out of pitchers, a position player takes the mound. Sure, there's a bullpen catcher to warm guys up, but he can't enter the game in an emergency.

In hockey, it could be an accountant, a Zamboni driver, an equipment manager, or a college kid who's studying for a big midterm. It's the most unique one-day job in sports and has provided a few of hockey's best real-life fairy tales over the past few years.

"It's so insane," Denver-based EBUG Justin Goldman said. "You can literally go from being Joe Schmo who plays beer league to stopping pucks in an NHL game and being the Man of the Year."

Foster, David Ayres, Jorge Alves, and countless others who put on an NHL uniform for a night can thank the inventors of the fastest game on ice for a position that's so specialized it would be downright dangerous for other players to strap on the pads and mask and try to stop a puck flying at them at 100 mph. Now they're household names for their 15 minutes—or less—of fame.

What happens when the only two goalies on a hockey team get hurt? Since 2015, the NHL has required each team to have a pool of emergency backup goaltenders at the ready should they or their opponent need one.

Since teams began dressing two goalies for a game in 1965, an EBUG has only gotten on the ice for real NHL action four times—all since New Year's Eve 2016 when Alves, the Carolina Hurricanes' longtime equipment manager, played the final 7.6 seconds in a lopsided loss at Tampa Bay.

"It doesn't matter if you play 8 seconds or half a game," Ayres said. "It's still pretty cool to be able to get into a game."

Foster played 14 minutes in Chicago, and Ayres—a 42-year-old Zamboni driver and arena operator at a nearby rink—became the face of emergency backup goalies when he took the ice for the Hurricanes against his hometown Toronto Maple Leafs in February 2020 and beat them on national television.

"It's smart. You've only got two goalies, so you've got to do something," he said. "I think it's cool. I kind of hope that someone else after me gets another chance and goes in and does the same thing—goes out there and shows everybody that there's guys that can jump in."

Two years later, life insurance salesman Tom Hodges played the third period of the Anaheim Ducks' game at the Dallas Stars on the final night of the 2021–22 NHL season.

It's the dream of every beer league goalie out there.

Somewhat amazingly, there has been wiggle room in the NHL rule book to make it possible for beer league goalies to play in the league. Rule 5.3 is open to interpretation:

> Each team shall be allowed one goalkeeper on the ice at one time. The goalkeeper may be removed and another skater substituted. Such substitute shall not be permitted the privileges of the goalkeeper. Each team shall have on its bench, or on a chair immediately beside the bench (or nearby), a substitute goalkeeper who shall, at all times, be fully equipped and ready to play. Except when both goalkeepers are incapacitated, no skater on the playing roster in the game shall be permitted to wear the equipment of the goalkeeper. In regular League and Playoff games, if both listed goalkeepers are incapacitated, that team shall be entitled to dress and play any goalkeeper who is eligible. In the event that the two regular goalkeepers are injured or incapacitated in quick succession, the third goalkeeper shall be provided with a reasonable amount of time to get dressed, in addition to a two-minute warm-up (except when he enters the game to defend against a penalty shot). If, however, the third goalkeeper is dressed and on the bench when the second goalkeeper becomes incapacitated, the third goalkeeper shall enter the game immediately and no warm-up is permitted.

"Any goalkeeper who is eligible" has taken on different meanings throughout hockey history. In the early days, another player—or coach—would take over. Sometimes it was a trainer or a house goalie waiting in the stands. As the goaltending position evolved into the specialized role it is as part of the modern game, it became necessary for someone with experience doing it to take over.

No, Ayres was not driving the Zamboni at the arena in Toronto and chosen at random to go into an NHL game. There wasn't a random lottery of fans in the stands to determine Foster would go in. EBUGs above all else are goalies, even if they did it at much lower levels of hockey.

"People think they're grabbing these EBUGs as guys who never put the pads on," Washington Capitals video coach and one-time emergency backup Brett Leonhardt said. "A Zamboni driver came in and won a hockey game in the NHL playing more than a full period—a team that needed those points to win a game."

The absurdity of that thought means the entire concept has some detractors. When Ayres allowed goals on the first two shots he faced, it looked bad. The Hurricanes were counting on a beer league goalie to win them a game in the middle of a playoff race.

"It's a cool story when you see it," longtime NHL goaltender Roberto Luongo said. "It's awesome. That one turned out OK, but sometimes these situations might not."

Much like a pitcher tossing a perfect game or a batter hitting for the cycle in baseball, the rarity of a hockey team needing an emergency backup is part of the charm. The fact that it wasn't needed for decades allowed for the chaos in Florida in 2015 when no one knew who could play and sparked a set of regulations to make sure that wouldn't happen again.

When Foster stopped all seven shots he faced to beat the playoff-bound Winnipeg Jets, there was nothing but amazement about the EBUG concept. Plenty of people weren't happy when

Ayres made eight saves against the Maple Leafs, but he became a national celebrity and shined a positive spotlight on hockey.

In the decade-plus since Tom Fenton dressed but didn't even play for the Phoenix Coyotes in 2010, he has gotten letters and cards from as far away as Slovakia. Each time he texts his buddies to tell them, "Legends never die." Perhaps that's the best part about the EBUG phenomenon: that it doesn't make any sense.

"I don't want to say it's laughable, but it's a fun part of sports— these weird stories that can come out of these serious games," Fenton said. "It's just fun."

CHAPTER 1

ORIGINS OF A TRADITION: HOW ONE-TIME GOALIES BECAME POSSIBLE

A S LONG AS HOCKEY has existed as a sport, goaltender has been the most important position with the chance to have the biggest impact on the game. Incredibly, for the first half of the 20th century, there was not much of a contingency plan in place if a goalie wasn't able to play for some reason during the course of a game. That could be as simple as the two or three minutes of a goalie serving his own penalty, which was the rule in the National Hockey League until 1949.

In the early years of the NHL, most teams only kept one goaltender on hand. The league had one house goalie to fill in as a substitute in the 1930s for long-term absences only. A rule was put in place in 1939 that a substitute stepping in net while a goalie serves a penalty could use a goaltender's stick and gloves but no other equipment—most notably leg pads.

By the 1941–42 season, the NHL made sure minor league goalies were on hand for emergency situations. Starting in 1950, every team was required to have an emergency goaltender in attendance with full equipment at each game for itself or its opponent to use in case of injury or illness. It wasn't until 1965 that teams were required to dress two goaltenders for each game.

NHL teams not having a backup, let alone a backup plan, led to plenty of memorable moments over the years of men who were not goaltenders stepping between the pipes.

According to league records, 21 non-goaltenders played the position in at least one game from 1919 to '60. Players in that era typically stayed on the ice for the whole game with spares around just in case.

"The guys that came on as the spare had to be utility-type guys," historian and author Liam Maguire said. "You had to be able to play any position. That was kind of a known thing. We look at it from a linear point of view today: if you're a defenseman, you've got to be a defenseman. If you're a left winger, you've got to be a left winger. Yeah, you had positions at that time, but it just wasn't as strict or as stringent as that."

The earliest occasion of a skater playing goal came on February 18, 1919, when Sprague Cleghorn of the original Ottawa Senators stepped in net for three minutes while Clint Benedict was serving a minor penalty. After penalties were reduced to two minutes for the 1921–22 season, Cleghorn went in goal for the Montreal Canadiens in a game against Ottawa when Georges Vezina was serving a penalty.

During a game at the Boston Bruins on March 15, 1932, Toronto Maple Leafs coach Dick Irvin tried goaltender by committee when starter Lorne Chabot was penalized, and it ended badly. King Clancy went in net and allowed a goal, Red Horner went in and allowed a goal, and then Alex Levinsky went in and allowed a goal, all on the same power play back in the day when the entire minor penalty had to be served. The Maple Leafs would have loved an emergency backup goalie that day because after giving up three goals in 91 seconds in the first period, they went on to lose 6–2.

Coincidentally, one of the referees that day was Sprague Cleghorn's younger brother, Odie, a forward who played one game in goal for the Pittsburgh Pirates in 1926. Odie Cleghorn allowed two goals over a full 60 minutes and beat the Montreal Canadiens. Only one skater has more wins as a goalie: defenseman Harry Mummery, who from 1920–22 allowed 20 goals in 192 minutes over four appearances and went 2–1–0.

The first instance of a player going in net during a playoff game happened in the 1923 Stanley Cup Final. King Clancy was a spare defenseman for the Senators at the time and was spelling Ottawa's five regular skaters—George Boucher, Punch Broadbent, Cy Denneny, Eddie Gerard, and Frank Nighbor—all over the ice during the best-of-three series against the Edmonton Eskimos.

When goalie Clint Benedict took a penalty, he handed his stick to Clancy while going off the ice and told him, "Look after the net until I get back." Clancy did not face a shot and with his two minutes in net became the first and only player in NHL history to play all six positions in the same game.

"He said, 'It's just no big deal at the time because goalies served penalties, so somebody had to go in net,'" said Maguire, who interviewed Clancy in 1983. "You look back now, and nobody did what he did."

Ottawa beat Edmonton 1–0 to take the best-of-three series 2–0 and win the Stanley Cup. It was the first of three Cup championships for Clancy, who played 16 NHL seasons for the Senators and Toronto Maple Leafs as a defenseman and was inducted into the Hockey Hall of Fame in 1958.

While Clancy's career in net lasted two minutes, the most famous instance of a substitute goaltender in the early days of the NHL came on April 7, 1928, in Game 2 of the Stanley Cup Final between the New York Rangers and Montreal Maroons. Montreal shut out the Rangers 2–0 two days earlier to take a lead in the best-of-five, and neither team scored in the first period of Game 2.

Twelve minutes into the second, a shot from Montreal's Nels Stewart struck New York goaltender Lorne Chabot in the left eye. It was bleeding bad enough that Chabot could not continue playing, and he ended up in Royal Victoria Hospital.

Rangers manager-coach Lester Patrick wanted to pluck star Senators goalie Alex Connell out of the stands at the Montreal Forum to finish the game, but Maroons manager-coach Eddie Gerard would not allow it. Gerard also turned down Patrick's attempt to dress minor league goalie Hugh McCormick. The Maroons were the only team at the time to carry two goaltenders, so Gerard said the Rangers should have also been prepared and had to put someone on their team in goal.

After some debate in the locker room, defenseman Leo Bourgault agreed to play, but teammates didn't like the idea of going down a skater.

"You've done everything in hockey, and you're still in pretty good shape," captain Frank Boucher said to Patrick, according to *Sports Illustrated*. "You can go in there yourself. We won't let them get a good shot at you."

While Patrick had a respectable career as a defenseman in various leagues across North America, he was a silver-haired 44-year-old at this point. Patrick agreed, slipping on Chabot's skates and equipment and going in net for the final 35 minutes. He told Odie Cleghorn, Pittsburgh's coach at the time, to run the bench for him.

Patrick was perfect until Stewart scored with 1:09 left in regulation. It went to overtime, and Boucher beat Maroons goaltender

Clint Benedict to even the series at a game apiece. Rangers players carried Patrick off on their shoulders.

Historian and author Eric Zweig said Patrick had gone in net a handful of times during his playing career, including in 1904 and 1906. In 1928, Patrick became the oldest player to appear in a Final.

"He'd actually done it quite a bit over the years, but not in the Stanley Cup Final at age 44," Zweig said. "The 1928 Stanley Cup Final is famous because a. it's the NHL and b. it's the Stanley Cup Final and he kind of heroically has to play quite a bit of that game."

With his heroics complete, Patrick went back behind the bench and the Rangers got permission to add goaltender Joe Miller, who played for the New York Americans that season. Miller allowed just three goals in three games the remainder of the Final, and the Rangers won the Stanley Cup in their second year of existence. Patrick coached the Rangers to another title in 1933 and was still manager when they won it all in 1940—the franchise's last Stanley Cup victory until 1994. He was part of the Hockey Hall of Fame's second induction class in 1947.

A few years removed from Patrick going in, league officials thought it would be a good idea to have a house goaltender available for all teams in case of injury. Wilf Cude signed to be the NHL's first utility backup goaltender on September 27, 1931.

"He was to make himself available at short notice to replace any other NHL goaltender that couldn't play for whatever reason," his son, Wilfred Lloyd Allan Cude, wrote in the book *Dear Red Light: Some Seasons in the Life of an NHL Goaltender.*

Cude played the previous season for the Philadelphia Quakers, but they folded, freeing him up for the league job. He mostly played in 1931–32 for the Boston Cubs of the Canadian American Hockey League but got into three NHL games in his unusual role. He posted a shutout in helping the Boston Bruins beat the New York Americans and two days later allowed six goals in a Bruins loss to the Toronto Maple Leafs.

His third game came by accident while he was with his fiancée, parents, and sister for a weekend in Toronto, where the Chicago Black Hawks were facing the Maple Leafs. Chicago goaltender Charlie Gardiner was twice knocked unconscious by a puck to the head. He stayed in the game the first time, but the second blow led to nine stitches, and doctors would not let Gardiner continue playing. (While Benedict wore a leather mask for a few games in 1930, goalies played maskless until 1959.)

Cude was summoned from the stands at Maple Leaf Gardens to take Gardiner's place late in the first period. Before the period ended, Cude was also struck in the face by a puck, impairing his vision and sending him to the locker room. Gardiner offered to go back in but was told he couldn't because he was scheduled to face Boston at home the following day. Cude returned to the ice to tend goal, which his son described as "squinting awkwardly at puck after puck ripping at him, feebly stopping what he could." He allowed nine goals, and the Maple Leafs beat the Black Hawks 11–3.

"And that was the less-than-glorious termination of his year's stint in the capacity of NHL back-up goalie," his son wrote. Wilf Cude went on to play 268 more games over eight seasons with the Montreal Canadiens and Detroit Red Wings. During that time, he backstopped Detroit to the 1934 Stanley Cup Final.

The strangest emergency goaltender situation in a Final happened in 1938, and historians differ on how much the circumstances were exaggerated.

Chicago goaltender Mike Karakas broke a toe in the semifinal-clinching victory against the New York Americans on April 3 at Madison Square Garden. With the Final beginning two days later in Toronto, the Black Hawks couldn't get minor leaguer Paul Goodman there on time and wanted to use Rangers goalie Dave Kerr, who lived in the area. The Maple Leafs said no and suggested Alfie Moore, who played the previous season for the Americans, was toiling in the minors, and was also a resident of Toronto. The search was on. Legend has it that Black Hawks players went to Moore's house the afternoon of Game 1 only to be told he was at a local tavern, and that the pursuit actually took them to a second bar before they found him.

"By the time Johnny Gottselig and Mush March, Doc Romnes, and these veteran guys had caught up to him, it was on the third bar," Maguire said. "The story goes he said, 'Holy jeez, am I ever glad to see you guys. I'm trying to get tickets to the game tonight.' They said, 'Alfie, you got no idea how good a seat you're going to have, buddy.'"

According to legend, players force-fed Moore coffee before the game started. They were none too happy when he allowed a goal on the first shot he faced less than two minutes in. But then Moore was perfect the rest of the way, and Chicago beat Toronto 3–1 to go up in the series.

Ty Dilello is one of the historians who does not believe the story of the Black Hawks finding Moore drunk in a bar.

"He was at his home," Dilello said, citing an interview manager Bill Tobin gave years later. "He wasn't actually drinking or drunk. I think that was just exaggerated to make it seem like, 'Oh, we picked up this guy off the street.' They might've said that to the Maple Leafs to allow them to use him."

Regardless of Moore's level of sobriety, Tobin paid him $300 for the effort and gave him a gold watch. League president Frank Calder declared Moore ineligible for Game 2 because he wasn't under contract, and Goodman was lit up 5–1 as the Maple Leafs tied the best-of-five series. Karakas had a steel boot inserted into his skate to protect his broken toe, returned for Games 3 and 4 and won them both to give Chicago the Stanley Cup. Moore got his name engraved on the trophy and only played one more NHL game the rest of his career.

Asked years later if he was actually drunk the day of the game, Moore said, "I had quite a few beers that day and I just can't remember."

Perhaps Moore was at his house and just returned from a bar, or maybe the entire thing was made up as a ruse. Maguire said he completely believes it, adding, "The Alfie Moore story, that's as good as there is."

But it was far from the last story of an emergency goaltender being called into action.

On November 27, 1943, the Boston Bruins were in Toronto when their only goaltender, Bert Gardiner, was too sick to play. Coach Art Ross asked the Maple Leafs for suggestions and was directed to their practice goalie, George Abbott, who doubled as a Baptist minister and whose playing career was ended by a puck to the eye.

Abbott was knocked out by a shot from Toronto's Babe Pratt but stayed in the game and allowed seven goals in a 7–4 Bruins loss. The Maple Leafs fared better against that practice goalie than they did 76-plus years later against another one.

When the first real EBUG system existed in the 1950s, it put Red Wings trainer Lefty Wilson in something of an awkward situation. It was no problem when he played 16 minutes in relief for Detroit when Terry Sawchuk was injured October 10, 1953. It was odd when he put on a Maple Leafs uniform and faced the Red Wings on January 22, 1956, and stopped all nine shots he faced by the team that employed him. Same thing on December 29, 1957, when he played almost the whole game for the Bruins and made 23 saves to preserve a tie against Sawchuk and the Red Wings.

That was just the job, and Wilson could clearly handle the assignment.

"In most cases, these guys had a smattering of goaltending experience," Maguire said. "You weren't going to the well and bringing in somebody who absolutely had never, ever, ever played net before."

A couple of years later, the Montreal Canadiens made sure they had someone with experience who was ready. They signed sportswriter Jacques Beauchamp to be their emergency backup goaltender on the road because he was always around them as part of his job covering the team.

The Canadian Press dispatch of November 19, 1959, read:

> Jacques Beauchamp, sports editor of the Montreal Matin and a fellow not without experience as a goalie, has been signed as a spare netminder with the Montreal Canadiens, it was learned Monday.
>
> The move came about because the National Hockey League club doesn't want to be called on to use a standby goalie in case of injury to goalie Jacques Plante on road trips.
>
> NHL regulations call for standby goalies in cases of emergency. But the standby frequently is scarcely even in the rookie class of minor-league or low-ranking amateur capacity.
>
> Beauchamp, 32, some years ago played with the junior A Montreal Concordias. He was the spare goalie for the Montreal Royals seniors when they won the Allan Cup 12 years ago. He had to give up regular practice workouts with Canadiens a few years ago because of his newspaper work but has continued playing in what he called the "depression league." It is an organization of former pro and amateur players.

> Beauchamp will continue reporting Canadiens' games.
> He would be used by Canadiens in a regular game only
> in case of emergency on a road trip.

Beauchamp never played for the Canadiens, though they named a prestigious team award after him.

Not long after Montreal tried to have its own backup plan on the road, Boston winger Jerry Toppazzini wasn't interested in wasting time for the emergency goalie to enter late in the Bruins' game at Chicago on October 16, 1960. Starter Don Simmons took a puck to the face off a shot from Black Hawks center Eric Nesterenko, which opened a cut under one of his eyes. Simmons couldn't continue, but with so little time left, Toppazzini went in net for the final 33 seconds. He didn't have to face a shot.

"Much like King Clancy, he just downplayed it," Maguire said, referring to a conversation with Toppazzini in 1999. "He said, 'It didn't really seem like that big a deal, plus, I was only in for 30 seconds.'"

The NHL went from Andy Branigan in 1941 until Toppazzini in 1960 without another skater filling in as a goaltender.

There have been scares since, including the spring of 2021 when Ottawa forward Artem Anisimov put on goalie gear and was set to go in if the Senators suffered a third injury at the position in a matter of hours, but Toppazzini remains the last position player to enter a game in net.

"It is sort of amazing," historian and author Eric Zweig said.

The league's final emergency backup goaltender before 1965 was Harrison Gray, who came out of the stands to fill in for Sawchuk when the Detroit Red Wings starter was injured on November 28, 1963. Gray allowed five goals on 31 shots in two periods of a 7–3 loss to the Montreal Canadiens at the old Detroit Olympia.

In the earlier days of hockey, and up until the late 1960s and early '70s, starting goalies played almost every game. Glenn Hall's 502 consecutive games played, 552 counting the playoffs, is a record that almost certainly will never be broken. It was just part of being a goalie.

"They'd never leave the game," Maguire said. "You were not getting these guys out of the net. They're not leaving."

Maguire said delays were commonplace so goalies could get a handful of stitches and stay in the game. Then the two-goalie system became the norm as the NHL expanded to 12 teams in 1967 and grew from there. Incredibly, from the time the two-goalie mandate started in 1965 until Scott Foster's appearance in 2018, the league went more than 45,000 games without an emergency backup entering a game.

Di Lello said it was a childhood dream of his and his buddies to get called out of the stands and play in a game.

"I always was kind of waiting for it to happen until the Scott Foster thing," he said. "I'm surprised both goalies haven't been hurt in one game. I couldn't believe it had been so long."

CHAPTER 2

THE ONE WHO MADE IT: CARTER HUTTON'S JOURNEY TO THE NHL

CARTER HUTTON went fishing with his dad as a child and told him he'd play for the Detroit Red Wings one day. That was Jack Hutton's favorite team, so naturally, it was Carter's dream.

When it was Carter's time to try goaltending, he fell in love with the equipment—the pads, the masks, and everything. He could wear something different than the rest of his teammates. When his father and a friend were coaching Carter's youth hockey teams, they argued over what position he should play. The friend won out, and Carter enjoyed every minute of strapping on new gear.

At age 14, he attended the International Ice Hockey Federation World Junior Ice Hockey Championships in Winnipeg, Manitoba, and watched Roberto Luongo tend goal for Canada. Russia beat Canada in the gold medal game, but that tournament made Hutton fall in love with the position even more and commit to being a goaltender.

Throughout his teenage years, Hutton tried out for the Thunder Bay Kings travel hockey team in his Ontario hometown every season. Every time, he was cut. A few times he acknowledged there were goaltenders who were better than him, and sometimes it was politics.

"It was his own fault to a certain degree because he was lazy when he was younger," said his father, Jack, who worked as a construction foreman in Thunder Bay. "They were just going through the motions."

"I wasn't really fit," Carter acknowledged. "I was a little chubby and didn't care about all that stuff."

After he was particularly stung by not making the Kings AAA team at age 17, Carter was sulking at the dinner table with his parents when his father reminded him of his dream of playing for the Red Wings.

"Carter, when you were seven or eight years old, it's all fine and dandy for you to dream of playing in the NHL," Jack told him. "That's wonderful. That's what kids are supposed to do. Beyond that now, you play hockey for what reason?"

"I play hockey because I love the game," Carter replied.

"Well, are you going to let these coaches for this Kings travel organization take that dream away from you?" Jack said. "If you win the Stanley Cup or if you win a cup from the local juvenile team, it's the same thing. It's the same game, and it's the same joy, so don't let them take that away from you. Go play for the love of the game. And if not that, play for your teammates. Don't go out there and give it a half-assed thing."

Carter dominated at the level he was forced to play at and by age 18 in 2003–04 he was playing the Tier 2 Superior International Junior Hockey League, which is not exactly a springboard to the NHL. However, it did turn out to be Hutton's jumping-off point to bigger and better things.

It was there that he met Gary Cook, a kingpin of junior hockey in Thunder Bay since he became involved with pro teams in 1967. Cook wasn't happy with Hutton's conditioning and felt like the young goalie's play was suffering as a result.

"He kind of ripped me," Carter said. "It lit a fire under me."

That conversation with Cook led to Hutton skipping a lot of his friends' parties and committing to doing more than just running stairs to get into shape. Whatever anxiety he developed about not working out enough fueled him to spend some extra time in the weight room.

"That was kind of when his game started to really take off," his father said. "He was always one of the primo goalies in this city, but he just didn't apply himself enough."

A trade up the standings to the Fort William North Stars in 2005 was the fortunate bounce Hutton needed. He won 31 games, set records—some that still stand, like five shutouts in a row—and backstopped them to the Dudley Hewitt Cup, which is the Ontario Junior A title, to qualify for the Royal Bank Cup, which is Canada's national championship at that level.

Almost every player there had a scholarship to play college hockey in the United States. Not Hutton—yet. Scouting in the stands at the Royal Bank Cup in Brampton, Ontario, was Jerry Forton, an assistant coach at the University of Massachusetts Lowell. The team needed a goalie, so Forton called head coach Blaise MacDonald and offered Hutton the chance to play in the NCAA's Division I.

"If you left that door open a crack, he'd kick it open," Jack Hutton said. "I've always called him the kid that wouldn't go away."

A few years later, Carter Hutton was the kid no one thought they'd ever see again. That was before he became the envy of every emergency backup goaltender around.

Hutton split the goaltending duties at UMass Lowell for much of his first three seasons there, to the dismay of his father and Uncle Don, who had done a lot of scouting and was a big fan of his nephew's game. Jack and Don Hutton even rented a place in Massachusetts to catch a bunch of Carter's games in the process.

"That was when my game really started coming together," Carter said of his time in college. Even though he believed he had more upside than the other goalies on the roster, he figured, "Wanting someone else to play badly so you can play, that doesn't do anything for me."

Hutton started 27 games to Nevin Thompson's 13 during his senior season and was clearly the No. 1 goalie. He won 12 games for the Riverhawks and ranked third in the nation with a .928 save percentage.

Somehow, he still did not have a pro contract offer. That is, until the Philadelphia Flyers called not long after his college season was over in March 2010. They immediately needed a goalie for their top minor league team, the Adirondack Phantoms. Director of scouting Chris Pryor, who watched Hutton play at UMass Lowell, wanted to sign him to a professional tryout.

Hutton, then 25 and far behind the usual development curve for goalies, was still taking classes at UMass Lowell to finish his finance and entrepreneurship degree. His mother, Linda, was a banker, so Carter believed "money makes the world go round" and felt it was important to set himself up for the future if hockey did not work out as planned.

He took a tryout deal to play in the American Hockey League with Adirondack on the weekends and was perfectly fine with that arrangement. A couple of his professors were insistent on Hutton taking exams and doing other schoolwork on time.

For a Canadian kid who thought playing professional hockey was the top of the mountain, Hutton found it hard to believe when professors didn't give him much of a break. It took some wrangling from the teacher who was assigned to help out the hockey team, and Hutton was able to work on his degree while advancing his goaltending career.

He played four games for the Phantoms from March 20 to 27, 2010, and stopped more than 92 percent of the shots he faced.

"We wound up beating Hershey," Hutton said. "Hershey was on some crazy win streak at home, and I was pretty naïve about that."

Hutton outdueled future Vezina Trophy and Stanley Cup winner Braden Holtby that night to snap the Bears' 24-game home winning streak, a few months before they won the Calder Cup as AHL champions.

A week later, he got a one-day cameo with the big club and his first taste of the National Hockey League, which very well could have been his last.

The Flyers were in the midst of an unprecedented run of injuries to their goalies. They'd finish the season dressing seven players at the position. They were especially desperate during the final weekend in March, when Swedish goalie Johan Backlund was injured—again—while playing in his first game of the season.

Brian Boucher was the only healthy goalie on the Flyers, so Pryor called Hutton's agent, Jordan Neumann, and signed him to an NHL tryout agreement so he could serve as a backup for a day.

"It came out of nowhere," Neumann said. "I had never had a player do that before in my career."

The night Backlund went down, Hutton was playing against the Manchester Monarchs—his second game in as many days. Hutton assumed the Flyers would promote 2005 draft pick Jeremy Duchesne, and they did a week later, but not then.

Phantoms coach Greg Gilbert summoned Hutton into his office and told him he was being called up to the Flyers. He needed to get to Philadelphia the next morning.

"I was taken aback," Hutton said. "The American League was a huge honor just to be playing there. The next morning, I flew out of Boston and met the team."

What followed was something Hutton never would have expected when he kept getting cut from teams as a teenager.

––––––––––

Hutton's head was still spinning when he was on the ice at the Wachovia Center in South Philadelphia for pregame warm-ups against the New Jersey Devils. It was less than 24 hours after he was told he was going to the Flyers, and on the other side of the ice was none other than future Hockey Hall of Famer and three-time Stanley Cup champion Martin Brodeur.

Hutton didn't feel like he belonged.

"I thought I was kind of a 'Make-a-Wish' kid," Hutton said. "I just lucked out, right time, right place."

Hutton took a sip of water and stared across the ice at Brodeur. He felt like a deer in the headlights.

"Why don't you ask him for an autograph?" one of the Flyers' athletic trainers said to him. Hutton put his head down and tried to concentrate.

He took his spot at the end of the bench while Boucher faced off against Brodeur, who was pulled after two periods for allowing four goals. Boucher joked to Hutton at the second intermission that he tweaked a knee, so he'd have to go in.

Boucher was fine, though with Philadelphia comfortably up 5–1 late in the third period, he skated over to the bench and offered to take a seat one more time.

"You want to get in here?" Boucher asked. Hutton looked at him in shock. He didn't move, and Boucher finished the game, a big win for the Flyers in the middle of a playoff race.

Before players could hit the locker room to celebrate, they stayed on the ice because it was fan appreciation night. A couple dozen season ticket holders would receive the players' jerseys.

Hutton thought that someone would get lucky and go home with Chris Pronger's jersey and another poor sucker would end up with his.

That poor sucker was John Demchuk. A season ticket holder since the Flyers' second season in 1968, he had never won anything of the sort. As he stood in the Zamboni tunnel holding a closed envelope that had a Flyers player's name written inside, he knew little of Hutton's story other than he had just been on the bench for his first NHL game.

Public address announcer Lou Nolan told Demchuk to open the envelope and read the name inside. "Carter Hutton," he said with some shock in his voice.

"The people who I sit with were looking through binoculars and they said, 'Oh, my God, the look on your face was unbelievable,'" Demchuk said.

Hutton nervously skated over and took the Sharpie from Demchuk. He didn't know what to do. Demchuk told him to turn it over and sign his autograph on the number 40. Hutton and Demchuk wished each other the best of luck and went their separate ways.

When Demchuk got home, he had a revelation: only one HUTTON 40 Flyers jersey existed on earth, and Carter should have the souvenir from his first NHL game. He wrote a letter to the Flyers to try to get the jersey back to Hutton and explained what led him to that decision.

Dear Carter,

My name is John Demchuk, a longtime Flyers season ticket holder since 1968. At Fan Appreciation Night on Sunday, March 28, 2010, you experienced a life-long dream to play for a team in the NHL—the Philadelphia Flyers as Brian Boucher's backup. What a thrill to put on NHL jersey, A FLYERS JERSEY, for the first time—even only for one game on an emergency basis as permitted by the NHL. You had to be excited to be given this opportunity. Ten days previously you were still a senior at the University of Massachusetts-Lowell. Dreams do come true. It was your lucky day on Sunday, March 28, 2010, to be at the Wachovia Center and be part of the Philadelphia Flyers organization as a player.

After the game that evening as part of Fan Appreciation Night, 26 fans were selected at random to receive the game-worn jerseys off the players [sic] backs. As you may recall, the players lined up at the blue line and the fans lined up behind the goal-line. Each fan was given an envelope to open after they were asked their name by the announcer and the player listed in the envelope skated toward the fan with jersey in hand to personally sign the number on the back of a jersey. I opened up my envelope and said over the loud speaker—CARTER HUTTON. As you skated toward me I saw that you were nervous and excited. I handed you my sharpie [sic] pen and you just shakingly tried to sign your name on the front of the sweater. I wished you good luck.

What an enjoyable and lucky evening for me to win a game-worn Flyers jersey. Never have I won such a prize since 1968. I was honored to have done so that evening.

While driving home, I realized that I had to contact someone at the Flyers to give back the jersey that you had worn as you dressed for your first NHL game. Any hockey player would want to keep that sweater as a memento of this joyous occasion. On Monday evening there was a season ticket holder event at the Wachovia Center and I spoke with Shawn Tilger, Senior Vice President of Business Operations for the Flyers, and he told me to call him on Tuesday, March 30, 2010. I did and I received a return phone call on Wednesday, March 31, 2010 and arranged that I will be dropping off your first game-worn NHL jersey on Friday evening, April 2, 2010 with the Flyers.

Hope you enjoyed your first tour of duty with the big club—even though it was only one game. Continued success with the Phantoms and hopefully your tryout contract will turn into a fullblown [sic] NHL contract in the future. Speaking of the future, I would like to meet you again one day when you are a little less nervous and excited. Maybe we can get together when the Phantoms come down to Philadelphia to play a regular season or a playoff game.

Good luck with your career and may God keep you in the palm of his hand.

Sincerely,

John C. Demchuk

LOYAL FLYERS FAN

Demchuk told Flyers owner Ed Snider that story in June while the team was facing the Chicago Blackhawks in the Stanley Cup Final. Snider insisted the team would get Demchuk a replacement game-worn jersey, and a few years later, he went home with one belonging to journeyman defenseman Nick Schultz.

When the season was over, Demchuk received a call. The voice on the other line said, "You don't know me, but I want to thank you."

It was Hutton's father, Jack, who was standing in front of the bright orange jersey framed and hanging on his living room wall with a message from Carter:

Mom & Dad
Thanks for Making
This all Possible
March 28, 2010

"That meant the world to me," Jack said. "It was the first NHL jersey he ever wore."

Eleven years later, Jack Hutton was again sitting in front of the jersey to talk about Carter. By that point, it was the first NHL jersey of many for a kid who, it turned out, really wouldn't go away.

Hutton never put on a Flyers or Phantoms jersey again. Pryor wanted Hutton to sign a minor league contract for the next season.

"They wanted me to go back and play in the American League," Hutton said. "I had established myself that I could get it done in the American League."

Philadelphia didn't have room to give Hutton an NHL contract because it had signed an intriguing Russian prospect named Sergei Bobrovsky. Neumann asked Pryor for some time to shop around for an NHL contract.

"If not, if we're going to do a minor league deal, we'll do it with you guys because we certainly want to be loyal for the opportunity you gave him, but give us an opportunity," Neumann told him.

Longtime San Jose Sharks assistant general manager Wayne Thomas was interested. He had done his homework on Hutton's tenure at UMass Lowell and his short stint in the AHL. On April 26, 2010, less than a month after his Flyers appearance, the Sharks signed Hutton to a one-year contract with a $60,000 signing bonus and $45,000 salary in the minors.

Hutton played in only 22 games that season for the Worcester Sharks, who had blue-chip prospect Alex Stalock as their No. 1 goaltender. San Jose had draft picks Harri Sateri and Tyson Sexsmith in the system, too, and Hutton did not get the chance to showcase himself for other NHL teams.

After the season, the interest in him dried up completely.

"He went from, 'Oh, my God, we're getting NHL contract offers' to, 'We have nothing' in just a matter of two, three months," Neumann said. "It went from 60 to 0 instead of 0 to 60."

As Jack Hutton likes to say, "That's the story of his life. Nothing ever came easy for him."

The next bend in the road took Hutton to Toledo, Ohio, to play for a low-level affiliate of the Chicago Blackhawks. He had signed a minor league deal that would let him play for the ECHL's Toledo Walleye and AHL's Rockford IceHogs.

"Most guys in that situation, they go to the ECHL, accept it's over and they play out the string," Neumann said.

Hutton figured all the disappointments as a kid and seeing other goalies have success motivated him not to play out the string. "I think it thickened my skin up," he said. It worked.

Hutton quickly became a staple in Rockford, and with the support of Blackhawks affiliate manager Mark Bernard, another NHL contract materialized for him in February 2012. He was called up for Chicago's playoff run to be a "Black Ace," an extra who practices with the team during the postseason. It was just another occasion for Hutton to realize how far he'd climbed.

During one practice, defenseman Duncan Keith asked Hutton if he'd ever played against a junior team called the Fort Frances Thunder. He had.

"At 16?" Keith asked. "At 20," Hutton replied.

Keith stopped dead in his tracks and said to Hutton, "And you're here."

Hutton didn't go anywhere, either. He signed another contract with the Blackhawks that summer—$80,000 in the minors this time—and made his NHL debut on April 27, 2013, a whole 37 months after he put on a Flyers uniform in Philadelphia.

Hutton made 25 saves on 28 shots that day and was along for the ride as a Black Ace when Chicago beat Boston to win the Stanley Cup that June. He played in 51 games for Rockford during the 2012–13 season but had only one NHL game on his résumé going into another summer without a contract. At any point, it could have been the end of the line.

Fortunately for Hutton, he had some of his best AHL games the previous year against the Milwaukee Admirals, the top minor league affiliate of the Nashville Predators.

"They couldn't shoot a bullet by him," Jack Hutton said.

The Predators had the best goaltending coach in the business on staff in Mitch Korn. When Dominik Hasek was working with Korn with the Buffalo Sabres, he won the Vezina Trophy as the NHL's best goaltender six times and the Hart Trophy as league MVP twice. He also helped Nashville's Pekka Rinne develop into one of hockey's best between the pipes.

Korn liked what he saw in Hutton without any real NHL experience. Korn wanted the team to sign Hutton to back up Rinne, who was the face of the franchise. Assistant general manager Paul Fenton called Neumann, who was plenty skeptical.

"You guys are a Cup-contending team. There's no way you're going to let your backup goalie be a guy that hasn't played," Neumann told him. The agent was convinced Hutton would be relegated to the minors once the Predators signed a veteran to pair with Rinne.

Fenton insisted the opportunity was real and said Hutton could prove what he could do. He signed his richest contract yet, one worth $550,000. As his dad pointed out, Carter Hutton never played in the AHL after that.

He played 40 games in 2013–14 while Rinne was out with a hip injury, and it wasn't all smooth. After allowing a soft goal on January 5 in a 2–1 loss at the Carolina Hurricanes, coach Barry Trotz ripped Hutton's performance as "not good enough in this league."

"We got zero saves," Trotz said.

Hutton bounced back and impressed Trotz in his next start nine days later, a 4–2 win at home against the Calgary Flames.

"I've always felt confident," Hutton told reporters that night. "You're a goalie and if you have a tough night or give up a tough goal, it falls on you. You battle back."

Hutton won 13 of 20 games and put up a 2.29 goals-against average and .917 save percentage following his rough game against Carolina.

"Instead of dropping his head and dropping his shoulders, from that point on, Carter played the best hockey of his life," Neumann said. "That's just always been the way he was. Any time anybody put adversity in front of him, he always raised his game."

It also raised his profile. Hutton earned his first multiyear deal, $1.45 million for two seasons, and established himself as a full-time NHL goaltender just shy of his 29th birthday. It was almost impossible to believe when he dressed as the Flyers' EBUG, even for Hutton himself.

"When he came, you don't think much of it. You're just like, 'Here's another guy,'" Boucher said. "To see him actually have a pretty lengthy NHL career is pretty cool. It's a lot of people's dreams to play in the NHL, and for him to play college and then get signed and turn it into a prosperous career is a cool story. I'm happy for him."

Neumann didn't even expect it after Hutton had finished his first NHL contract.

"When he signed the East Coast League contract with Toledo, at the time, if you would've told me this guy's going to have a 10-year NHL career, I would have told you you're crazy," he said.

Hutton went from the Predators to the St. Louis Blues and became fully entrenched in the NHL. He led the league with a .931 save percentage in 2017–18, which earned him a three-year contract worth $8.25 million with the Buffalo Sabres. An injury cut short his time with Buffalo, and Hutton signed with the Arizona Coyotes in the summer of 2021.

By the end of the 2021–22 season, he had amassed career earnings of more than $12 million and played in more than 200 NHL games.

No one saw that coming. Not even Hutton.

"If I'm being totally honest, no, I never thought that," he said. "Each level I've gone to, I've kind of adapted and done what I've needed to do. I just kind of kept chipping away at it."

Hutton knows he's the envy of every EBUG who has ever gotten close to putting on an NHL uniform. Along the way, he tried to pay some of his lessons forward.

On October 18, 2016, when Ryan Miller was unable to dress for Vancouver, the Canucks called on University of British Columbia goalie Matt Hewitt to back up Jacob Markstrom against Hutton and the Blues. Hutton congratulated Hewitt during warm-ups and wished him the best.

"He said something cheeky like, 'You're getting lucky tonight,'" Hewitt recalled.

"I usually tell guys, 'Wear your jersey to the bar tonight,'" said Hutton, who always liked to keep it light with kids who were getting their first opportunity in the NHL because he remembered what it was like.

Some of the conversations were more sentimental. Recalling how longtime Sharks captain Joe Thornton welcomed him with open arms when he got called up to San Jose, Hutton wanted to pay it forward.

"It is very surreal, but make sure you soak it in but still work hard and you never know," Hutton said. "It's such a unique situation where you get a guy, just a local guy or someone in the area that can play to be up there and you're one situation away from stepping on the ice to play in the NHL."

Hutton played his part, too. The next season, he went down with injury and Blues practice goaltender Tyler Stewart got his moment in the limelight by taking warm-ups on December 7, 2017.

"I tried to talk to him and tell him things not to do, just so you fit in," Hutton said. "Kind of like when Happy Gilmore is teeing off and he stands right in front of the guy and he's ready to hit his first drive—just don't do anything to make yourself look too stupid."

Hutton knows that from experience, like not to do anything to cause trainers to make fun of you.

"Guys that are emergency call-ups are kind of just randomly making it," Hutton said. "It's a bit more overwhelming. You're kind of just thrown into the spotlight. I've always tried to be aware of that and aware of what that does to a person. I know what it feels like."

Demchuk tried to imagine what it felt like to be Hutton, a player in an NHL uniform for the first time, when he decided to send the jersey back. Hutton never returned to Philadelphia with the Phantoms but made good on meeting up with Demchuk after the Predators played the Flyers on January 16, 2014.

"He was very, very thankful and we've kept a texting relationship ever since," Demchuk said. "He was so calm and so thankful, and he really appreciated it. It meant something more to him than it did to me."

Hutton stopped 27 of 30 shots in regulation and overtime that night, then five more in the shootout to beat the team that he suited up for but never signed him beyond that day. Demchuk continued to text Hutton before every game against the Flyers and when Hutton's children were born.

"I said, 'I'm your No. 1 Flyers fan from Philadelphia,'" Demchuk said. "I'm really proud of him and I'm really happy to follow his story. What an incredible story. This is a guy that worked hard for many, many years to make it to where he is."

For Neumann, there are few prouder accomplishments in his years representing players than Hutton, who he tells often, "What you've done is amazing."

Jack Hutton knows that, too. He hopes his own encouragement along the way helped but also believes Carter's attitude kept him in the NHL well into his thirties as much as his play on the ice.

"A big part of how he's stretched his career into nine or 10 years is his personality," he said. "They want people like that in their dressing rooms nowadays. It's so important. The NHL is a lot of peaks and valleys, and you can't start whining at that level."

Since that night at the dinner table in the early 2000s, Hutton rarely whined about his place in hockey.

"I always believed in myself," he said. "I think I just kept progressing. I kind of used each step as a stepping-stone."

Beyond being a hero of the EBUG community, Hutton is an example for late-blooming goalies not to give up on trying to make it to the NHL. He has tried to use his own story of being cut from travel teams and underestimated at various stops as a lesson for younger players and teammates.

"It's not always that young star, drafted high, best player in junior. You can make it other ways," he said. "I pride myself on vocalizing that story to kids so they know, just because you got cut, it's not the end of the world, too, and I think I benefited from it."

In the "back nine" of his NHL career playing for Arizona during the 2021–22 season, Hutton concedes, "It's been kind of a wild ride."

"Who knew?" he said. "I always say to my dad or my buddies, 'Whoever would have thought I'd play this long and have this kind of success?' It's obviously nuts."

After visiting Carter, his wife, Stacy, and their children in Arizona, Jack and Linda Hutton missed their connection in Toronto on the way back home to Thunder Bay. It was not a good day, so Jack wanted a beer and went down to the pub in the hotel around midnight.

Sitting there was a trading card collector from Wainwright, Alberta, in a Flyers jersey who introduced himself and quickly realized, "You're Carter Hutton's parents." He knew everything about Hutton's career and was missing only his Score "Hot Rookie" card in the Flyers uniform. When Jack Hutton returned home, he put a signed rookie card in the mail to complete the collection of a career few people thought Carter would have.

"He has earned everything," Jack said. "He has gotten a couple of breaks along the way. I think you have to be in the right place at the right time as well."

CHAPTER 3

CHAOS IN FLORIDA:
BACK FROM THE HOSPITAL
TO SAVE THE DAY

Roberto Luongo could sense the chaos from the hospital seven miles away.

The Florida Panthers starting goaltender was waiting for the results of an X-ray on his right shoulder and started scrolling through Twitter on his phone to keep up with his team's game against the Toronto Maple Leafs that he left with the injury. Backup Al Montoya, who had entered as his replacement, went down in pain after being scored on early in the third period and was too hurt to continue playing.

The game stopped for almost 10 minutes because no one knew who was going to play goal for the Panthers. Luongo had seen speculation that forward Derek MacKenzie was strapping on the goalie pads and that goaltending coach Robb Tallas could enter the game.

Oh my god, what the hell's going on? Luongo thought to himself.

When the doctor returned from the clinic with the results that showed a broken bone in his right shoulder, Luongo said they needed to hurry back to the arena. By the time he returned, Montoya had allowed a goal while playing through a torn groin muscle and the Panthers were losing a game they desperately needed to win to keep pace in the Eastern Conference playoff race.

Luongo put his gear back on and finished the game. Months later, the NHL put together a plan so nothing like this would happen again.

The Panthers woke up on March 3, 2015, two points back of the Boston Bruins for the second and final wild-card spot in the East. Luongo was starting for the 52nd time in 64 games.

Montoya wasn't feeling right in the time leading up to the game against the Maple Leafs. He saw the chiropractor before the game to line everything up and put a heat pack on his legs to maintain his groin muscles. More or less, he was trying to keep his body together.

With Montoya watching from the bench as the backup, Luongo stopped the first 13 shots the Maple Leafs put on net with no issue. Almost 16 minutes into the first period, Toronto's Leo Komarov skated down the left wing and fired a seemingly harmless shot from a sharp angle just below the goal line. Luongo sealed the post and opened himself up for a bad break.

He leaned into the shot and the puck hit him square in the back of the shoulder just at the point where a goalie's chest protector stops and there's no real padding. It stung him immediately, and Luongo went down in the crease. Referee Justin St-Pierre blew the whistle even though the play was live.

Luongo reached for his right shoulder and rolled onto his back while head athletic trainer Dave Zenobi rushed over to attend to him.

"I wasn't sure exactly what had happened, but I was in some pain," Luongo said. "I could barely raise my arm."

He tried. With Zenobi watching closely, Luongo tried to raise his right arm over his head, grabbed the goal post, and flexed his shoulder. Something didn't feel right, so he left the ice and went down the tunnel to get it looked at.

"At the time, Lou never got hurt," Montoya said. "He comes off the ice and you're like, 'OK, this has got to be serious.'"

Montoya was worried about Luongo and at the same time thought this was his chance to show what he could do. "I jump in the net, I'm ecstatic, ready to go," he said. Montoya entered the net with 4:03 remaining in the first period.

Luongo didn't think he had broken a bone, but initial X-rays showed something wrong, so the decision was made for a doctor to take him to the Cleveland Clinic, a 15-minute drive away, for some clearer images.

Brandon Pirri gave the Panthers a 1–0 lead with 18 seconds left in the first. Montoya didn't face a shot before the first intermission. He allowed a goal to Tyler Bozak that tied it early in the second, and Florida went on top again when Aaron Ekblad scored and led 2–1 after two periods.

Everything changed in the first minute of the third.

———

Toronto defenseman Jake Gardiner's shot went wide to Montoya's left and took a hard bounce off the end boards and out in front to forward Nazem Kadri, who was crashing the net. Montoya stretched out and slid to try to stop Kadri, but the puck got by him into the net. It was 2–2 just 22 seconds into the third period, but the Panthers had bigger problems.

Montoya knew immediately he had torn his left groin muscle. He kept stretching it out and was noticeably uncomfortable in the crease. With St-Pierre checking in on Montoya, veteran Florida forward Brad Boyes talked to the injured goalie, and teammates Erik Gudbranson and Nick Bjugstad soon joined the conversation. Montoya coasted to the bench with most of his weight on his right skate to have a word with Zenobi. He motioned that something went wrong while doing down in the split to try to make the save.

Montoya skated back to his crease and back to the bench, and the confusion was just beginning.

Referee Dave Jackson approached the Panthers bench and asked, "What are you going to do here?" Coach Gerard Gallant responded, "Tell me what we can do."

"Fuck if I know," Jackson said. The veteran referee knew all about the rule that if both goalies were incapacitated a team could dress a substitute. But there was no clear definition of what that meant.

"It never came to that," Jackson said years later. "The second goalie was always going to be good, or the first goalie would come back in, and it was never really addressed."

Montoya was not feeling up to staying in the game, and there was no obvious solution. St-Pierre skated over to the penalty box, put on the headset, was put in touch with the situation room in Toronto, and was told they'd have to get back to him with an answer. Montoya left the ice and went down the same tunnel Luongo had a couple of hours earlier.

"It's just a freak thing," general manager Dale Tallon said. "It doesn't happen very often, and you're not prepared for that."

As such, there was not a backup goalie sitting on the bench.

"What really should have happened, we should have stopped the game," Tallas said. "The refs should have stopped the game, allowed 20 minutes to kind of regroup and sort it out."

There was no precedent for this. Since the NHL required teams to dress two goaltenders for each game beginning in 1965, no team had both goalies incapacitated during the same game. The rulebook offered only general guidance about the ability to insert a substitute in net. That only added to the uncertainty.

"It was very frustrating," Jackson said. "Everybody was kind of in the same boat. The team didn't know what to do. We call the situation room and the situation room, they're not the New York player registry. They're a bunch of ex-players and ex-officials making determinations on rules."

Amid the confusion, Tallas rushed down from the press box. On the verge of turning 42, Tallas played 99 NHL games from 1996 to 2001 and had tended goal professionally as recently as 2005. Exactly two years earlier, he dressed as the Panthers backup for warm-ups and the start of a game until call-up Jacob Markstrom's equipment arrived.

The situation room told St-Pierre that because Tallas was not on the active roster, he could not play. Jackson delivered the bad news to Gallant at the bench and told him: "If you want a little more time, we'll just take some time here and you can figure things out. We'll wait. If you want 5, 10 minutes, we'll just wait."

The Panthers were of the understanding that they needed to dress a skater or go without a goaltender.

"There was a lot of stuff going on," Gallant said. "Nobody was really sure what we could do. At one point we just said, 'Well, we'll play with six players the rest of the game, and that's what we were going to do.'"

Playing more than 19 minutes with no goaltender? Not ideal. Forward Derek MacKenzie joked that since he was the worst player, he'd go in net.

"I wasn't keen on that," Gallant said. "I don't like to put a player in a situation where he can get hurt."

There weren't many options available. Gallant asked MacKenzie if he was sure. MacKenzie wasn't thinking at all about a potential injury and responded, "I'll do it. I'll go in."

MacKenzie hustled down the tunnel to gear up. There was still no clarity on what was happening, and the game was still delayed. "It seemed like forever," Tallon said.

"What a bizarro night," team president Peter Luukko said.

Luongo only knew what was happening because he checked his phone while awaiting the results of his X-ray. There was a small fracture in his right shoulder, but it wasn't anything that couldn't wait. After finding out what was wrong, Luongo told the doctor they needed to hurry back to the rink as soon as possible.

They got back on the road and rushed back. Luongo was still on Twitter trying to decipher the developments unfolding at the arena, just like everyone else.

"There was so much confusion, and nobody knew what was going on," he said.

MacKenzie had gotten to the locker room and figured Tallas' equipment would fit him better than Luongo's or Montoya's. He took off his forward gear and started strapping on the goaltending gear. He had the pads on and the upper-body protection. There was only one problem—his jersey wouldn't fit over the chest and shoulder pads because it wasn't goalie sized.

While waiting for a jersey, MacKenzie had all these thoughts race through his mind. He knew sharpshooter Phil Kessel was on the other side and thought about how he would stop a rapid-fire one-timer.

"I have no idea what I'm going to do," MacKenzie said. "If I sell it, if I go out on the ice and shuffle the crease and tap my posts, maybe they don't exactly figure out what's going on and they don't go out of their way to take shots. Maybe I can fool them a little bit."

MacKenzie would have been the first skater to play goal in the NHL since Jerry Toppazzini in 1960. He took some shots in net years earlier in the minors and figured he couldn't play a modern style but would try to get the job done as an old-school, standup goalie.

MacKenzie thought to himself, *You've got one trick up your sleeve and that's stack the pads, and you can't even do that very good. Just get in there and hope.*

Tallas arrived on the chaotic scene and gave MacKenzie a weird look. Tallas told him, "You can't get dressed. I know for a fact *you* can't get dressed. The only guy that can get dressed right now is me."

MacKenzie went from thinking he was making his NHL goaltending debut to putting his regular equipment back on. Tallas began his preparations to play. He knew Luongo was on his way back from the hospital, but he didn't know how much time was left in that trip.

By this point, the situation room called the on-ice officials back and told them that Tallas *was* eligible to play if he signed a one-day contract. Behind the scenes, the Panthers had gotten the same answer.

Tallon and owner Vinnie Viola were in the thick of the discussion trying to figure out what to do and what was legal. The team called Commissioner Gary Bettman to expedite the process and make sure Tallas could enter the game. They were told he could as long as he signed the contract.

Sitting in the locker room putting on his equipment and awaiting word, Tallas' biggest worry was stepping on the ice in goalie skates. After moving into coaching, he switched to forward skates and did not know how this would go.

"My first three or four strides were going to be hard," Tallas thought. "Imagine if I fall? Just get to your net with your skates. You've got to get the balance under your feet first. You've got to get to your net safe."

Tallas never got to test that out.

Montoya was in the locker room amid the chaos of MacKenzie trying to get dressed and team officials buzzing around working on plans C, D, and maybe E. He knew his groin was torn, but the arena didn't have an MRI machine that would have shown it.

Montoya's thoughts went from, *I'm about to take over the net for the next however long* to, *Crap, if I continue playing this game, I might be out for another full year.*

The Panthers didn't have another clear option. Gallant looked at Montoya and asked, "Can you go?" Montoya agreed, put his mask back on, and got back on the ice. After all the wacky scenarios and the time spent, Montoya stayed in the game.

Luongo returned from the Cleveland Clinic to see Tallas putting on his gear.

"I looked at his face and he was white as a ghost," Luongo said. "I said, 'I can't let this guy do this.'"

Tallas had signed the professional tryout contract that allowed him to get into uniform, just in case. Luongo tried to convince the management and medical staffs to let him go back in the game. He figured he could do a better job of trying to stop shots than Montoya, who could barely move. It was an important game, and Luongo knew he could move.

"The only thing I can't do is I can't lift my arm," he said. "At least I can skate and go butterfly and do the movements I needed to do to at least try to get my body in the way of shots."

Tallon didn't know the extent of Montoya's injury, and he sure didn't want Luongo to get hurt any more. "We didn't want to lose our big guy," Tallon said.

After a few minutes of conversation, Luongo got the green light. He rushed back to the locker room to change out of his suit and back into uniform.

While he was doing that, Tallas got to the bench with a jersey, a mask, and gear on to watch the action and step in if needed.

Montoya was still in net and made four saves in his first two minutes on the ice. A few shifts later, Toronto's David Booth put the puck on net and Peter Holland knocked in the rebound to take a 3–2 lead with 14:32 remaining in the third.

Montoya could not go down in the butterfly stance because of his groin, so he was helpless to stop the second shot, and the Maple Leafs knew it.

"I think if he was feeling 100 percent, he would have gotten across the net there," Holland said. "That's not typical Montoya. He's usually pretty quick along the bottom there. They don't ask how, and I won't ask how, either."

Midway through the period, Luongo had his gear on and was back at the bench. When the whistle blew with 9:08 left, he opened the bench door, skated over to the crease, gave Montoya a tap, and relieved his badly injured teammate.

"That's that," Montoya said. "I come to find out that night, when I sit down, I couldn't even stand up. I never had a groin injury like that before."

Montoya missed the next five weeks before returning for the regular season finale. Six years later, he could still feel where the injury happened.

For the rest of that game, it was Luongo's net. MacKenzie said, "When he got back, it kind of all fell into place."

Luongo faced only three shots and stopped them all, and the Panthers put 17 attempts on Maple Leafs goaltender Jonathan Bernier.

"I think I might've played the puck once or twice," Luongo said. "We were pressing the last seven or eight minutes, so I didn't really have to use my arm, and it was fine."

Bernier stopped all those third-period shots by Florida, and the Maple Leafs snapped a franchise-worst 16-game road losing streak with their first victory away from home since December 31.

"It was unfortunate we let this one slip away," Pirri said after the game. "These are two big points we needed."

Gallant added, "We're playing a pretty good game, and all of a sudden, boom, boom, you lose two goalies real quick."

Losing their goalies had a lasting effect on the Panthers. Montoya was on the shelf long term, and Luongo missed six games over the following two weeks. Florida went 3–2–1 with replacement Dan Ellis in net. By the time Luongo returned, the Panthers were seven points back of the final playoff spot with 12 games left.

They couldn't pin it all on losing on March 3, but there was plenty of justified second-guessing going on.

"Putting our goalie coach in at the time would've been a way better solution from a game standpoint," MacKenzie said. "Robb Tallas can go in and look like an NHL goalie. It would've worked out fine. Obviously a different style, different time, but he would have given us the best chance to win at that time. But it just didn't materialize that way."

While the debate was going on, the Panthers didn't have much of an idea Luongo could come back. No one called him, and it wasn't until he notified the team that he was on his way that there was much hope.

"Lou the competitor comes up, and you feel bad as a goalie because your job is to be there when he can't," Montoya said. "All that stuff is the competitor in you. I'm just grateful that we had an option and that he was OK."

MacKenzie felt a sense of disbelief as the entire debacle was unfolding. He wondered just how close he was—maybe if the jersey fit? If Luongo was stuck in traffic for five minutes longer?—to going in the game as a goaltender.

"What are the odds that all that fell into place?" he said. "There's a lot of ways that could've went. You're going into this like, 'I've got nothing to lose,' in a sense. What a story to tell. But at the same time, it was a close game, and I didn't want to go in and be so bad that I really blew it. In hindsight, it would've been messy."

The entire situation was messy, and Tallas said "it definitely sent a message to the league to clarify the emergency backup position from that point forward." When the situation happened later in March to the Bruins, fellow retired goalie Bob Essensa dressed as the backup with far less madness and fanfare.

Despite the rarity of two goaltenders going down in the same game, hockey had changed and there was more of an emphasis on skaters crashing the net and creating traffic in front.

"Especially at the speed of the game that we play at—the way players attack that net, there are more collisions," Montoya thought. "Even though I knew it was an odd situation, I knew it wasn't the last time it was going to happen."

General managers and league hockey operations staff hammered out a plan that led to each team preparing a list of emergency backup goaltender options for every game. It all stemmed from the Florida fiasco.

"We had to, because that was a real emergency," Tallon said. "Emergencies happen quickly. If you don't have a plan in place, it's hard to do anything that's correct."

Luukko said the night "showed a little bit of a flaw we have in the game."

"The goalie is such an integral part of the game," he said. "To have a good legitimate competition, the goalie is so essential to that. There could be one school of thought—'Well, if they both go down, that's part of the game. You got to just deal with it.' But it's probably more important if you can find and have access to someone who's actually played the position."

The NHL eventually figured it out. The Panthers took a pro-active step to see who might be out there.

CHAPTER 4

THE AUDITIONS:
HOW TEAMS PICK THEIR
EMERGENCY BACKUPS

N OT ALL NHL emergency backup goaltenders are chosen equally. The Chicago Blackhawks found Scott Foster by calling the owner of a local hockey rink asking about beer league goaltenders. The Colorado Avalanche asked Goalie Guild founder and local house goalie Justin Goldman who the top options were in the Denver area. The Toronto Maple Leafs rotated among three local universities and practice goalie David Ayres.

In the aftermath of their goaltending fiasco on March 3, 2015, the Florida Panthers came up with an idea to capitalize on the spotlight that was already on them. The day after injuries to Roberto Luongo and Al Montoya plunged the team's game into a lengthy delay over uncertainty about who was going to go in net, executive chairman Peter Luukko was talking to assistant coach John Madden about possibilities. Madden brought up the emergency backup goalie tryouts the Minnesota Wild used to hold, and Luukko set in motion the plan to try that for the Panthers.

On March 5, the announcement went out for the "Goal of a Lifetime" contest:

The "Goal of a Lifetime" contest is open to all men and women goaltenders (must be 18-years-old [sic] or older). All goaltenders are asked to submit their playing resume to FloridaPanthers.com/backupgoalie. After reviewing the resumes, a select group of goaltenders will participate in an on-ice try-out that will take place on Monday, March 16, at 4 p.m. at BB&T Center. Panthers Goaltending Coach Robb Tallas and select Panthers Alumni will oversee the try-outs.

Two finalists will be selected from the try-outs and will be invited to compete in a shootout that will feature Panthers Alumni during the first intermission of Florida's game against Montreal on March 17. The goaltender with the best performance in the shootout will be selected as the Panthers' back-up practice goalie.

It was like a bat signal with a goalie silhouette. The team received more than 1,500 applications from 15 different countries and 42 U.S. states.

"We had people from so many countries emailing us and sending in submissions and wanting to try out and willing to put their jobs on hold and travel from so far," Tallas said. "As far as Japan and Australia, we were being contacted by people to come to the tryout. So it became a pretty global thing."

———

Bill Ruggiero was running a surf shop and grill in St. Croix in the U.S. Virgin Islands when he saw a Facebook post about the tryouts. By this point, he was better known in hockey as the brother of U.S. women's hockey star defenseman Angela Ruggiero, who later in 2015 was inducted into the Hall of Fame. But he enjoyed quite the life in hockey before hanging up his goalie pads.

Angela and Bill Ruggiero grew up playing together in Southern California in the mid to late 1980s before Wayne Gretzky was traded to the Los Angeles Kings and the sport began blossoming in the state. Their father, Bill, had been a stick boy for a semi-pro team in Florida, got some goaltending equipment out of it, and became a goalie for life. His son followed those footsteps and played goal wherever he could find the ice.

"Playing in California was tough because if you want to play really competitive [hockey], you have to travel," he said. "So I was always on the road, and that takes a toll on your family. I was traveling at least twice a month out of state to play."

A couple of fellow locals made it to the NHL: Noah Clarke and Garrett Stafford. Bill certainly tried. While Angela starred in high school at Choate Rosemary Hall in Wallingford, Connecticut, on the way to becoming the youngest member of the gold-medal-winning U.S. team at the 1998 Nagano Olympics, he moved to Michigan at age 15 to play competitively at the Triple A level and spent a year with the Kingsville Comets of the Great Lakes Junior C Hockey League.

The same year his sister won Olympic gold, Bill Ruggiero was drafted at age 17 into the Ontario Hockey League, the highest level of junior hockey, and played 21 games over two seasons with the London Knights and Plymouth Whalers. He moved on to play 68 games for the Moncton Wildcats of the Quebec Major Junior League and in 2001 got a taste of the NHL by attending a camp with the Nashville Predators. He did not get a contract offer, but Ruggiero left with plenty of confidence based on how many stops he made at camp.

Ruggiero played games in 2001–02 in the QMJHL, Maritime Junior Hockey League, North American Hockey League, and East Coast Hockey League. In the following seasons, he bounced around the minors playing for teams like the Tulsa Oilers of the

Central Hockey League, the Motor City Mechanics of the United Hockey League, and the Flint Generals of the International Hockey League. He starred for a team in Finland in 2008–09, and that summer at age 28 looked to be bound for the Russian-based Kontinental Hockey League. That deal fell through at the last minute, leaving Ruggiero floating.

In 2009–10, his four games in the All American Hockey League with the Detroit Hitmen were his last in organized pro hockey.

"I was playing well and being a goalie," he said. "I pretty much left home at 15 to play hockey, so I was kind of 15 years on the road. But I was still hungry and obviously I loved the sport."

Ruggiero had moved on from hockey as a career to growing his own business in St. Croix that catered to cruise ship passengers and tourists. He saw the post about the Panthers goalie tryouts in the wee hours of the morning and thought it might be a way back in at age 34. He sent in an application, and before it was even received, he flew to Michigan to begin preparations. He bought a new glove and blocker and got on the ice a handful of times while waiting to hear back.

"It was a total chance that I took," he said.

With the understanding that the contest winner needed to be a legal resident of Florida, Ruggiero met up with a friend who lived there, got a driver's license, and put his name on a lease. Turned out that by the day of the tryouts there was no residency requirement, but Ruggiero was all in.

Ruggiero was one of 65 goalies invited to the tryout on March 16. Of the 58 men and women who showed up at BB&T Arena, five came from Canada and 48 were Florida residents. That counted Ruggiero.

Linda Cohn didn't get the award for the furthest distance traveled, but she was there front and center. The *SportsCenter* anchor knew all about the Panthers goalie fiasco and pitched participating in the tryout to one of her bosses at ESPN. Cohn was a goaltender growing up, playing with the boys in high school because there wasn't a girls team, before moving on to women's hockey in college at Oswego State.

"Besides their great sunsets and their great communications program, it was because they had a women's hockey team," Cohn said. "That's why I picked them."

Cohn was famously a New York Rangers fan, but she didn't think most viewers knew her hockey-playing background of tending goal at Oswego State from 1977–81.

"First and foremost, deep down in my heart I'm like maybe I can open up some eyes," she said. "I don't think they really know that I played goal and what it takes to play this position and explaining why it makes me a little nutty. But that's the way I am."

It had been a while since Cohn spent any time in net, so she arrived a day early and got in an on-ice workout with former Panthers goaltender Tomas Vokoun. She said Vokoun told her, "Linda, I know you know this, but remember, Goalie 101: always keep your stick on the ice." It all clicked back into place for Cohn, who went live the next day on *SportsCenter*.

"I'm so competitive and I didn't want to embarrass myself," she said. "I felt like I was representing a lot of people and I didn't want it to be just a PR stunt, a sideshow—all of the above."

Cohn faced shots from Panthers forward Shawn Thornton as part of her tryout. Thornton's first shot from the left faceoff circle whistled by her left shoulder. She stopped the next 11 shots she faced, but at 5'5" and 56 years old, she did not expect to get chosen as one of the finalists.

"There were more qualified female goalies there," said Cohn, who called it one of the happier moments of her career. "They were good. We were all pinching ourselves, the experience of, 'Hey, could this happen? This is amazing. I can't believe I'm here.'"

Talent ranged from former professionals with recent experience to one-time recreational league goalies who hadn't put on pads in 20 years.

"I could tell there was a variety of athleticism and ability," Ruggiero said. "You could tell there was a few guys there that played Division III and guys that played who you could tell were pretty good."

Dustin Smith was definitely one of the pretty good ones. After goaltending in high school in Nashville and playing college club hockey from 2006–09 at Middle Tennessee State, he started practicing with the Predators during the 2012–13 NHL lockout. The 27-year-old skated with Nashville players during summer workouts and occasionally during the season.

Smith saw the game when the Panthers ran out of healthy goaltenders and heard about the competition they were holding. His Southwest Airlines coworkers at the Nashville airport said they'd fill out an application for him, but Smith was worried they'd butcher it, so he filled out one himself and was thrilled to be accepted. He flew to South Florida with no expectations.

"I knew it was going to be kind of a clinic-style thing with stations everywhere," Smith said. "I just went to go down there to jump on the ice and kind of have a good time and run through some drills."

Tallas was in charge of those drills. He had run plenty of summer goalie camps and had an idea what kind of paces to put the contestants through.

"I actually skated them quite hard at the beginning, put them through a whole day of testing and stuff like that and just kind of narrowed it down to who we felt was the best goalie on the ice," Tallas said. "A lot of people came in knowing that they had no chance and then there was a few people that came in saying that they had a real good chance at it."

Ruggiero knew Montoya a little from workouts back in Michigan when the onetime top NHL prospect played college hockey there and they skated together during the summer. He was also Vokoun's goaltending partner at Predators camp in 2001 and figured he had a chance.

Vokoun, Luukko, and Tallas were among the judges who ultimately picked Ruggiero and Smith to face off in a shootout during the first intermission of Florida's game against the Montreal Canadiens the next night, March 17.

"It was so much fun being on the ice and being able to try out," Smith said then. "Obviously exhausting. They put us through the wringer."

With the shootout being shown live on the Panthers television broadcast, Smith and Ruggiero took shots from former NHL forwards Marco Sturm and Radek Dvorak. Each stopped three of four shots, and in a throwback to life before the shootout in the NHL, it was declared a tie.

"I just tried to go down there and have a lot of fun," Smith said. "And things just kind of ended up working out."

The Panthers went in looking for one emergency backup goalie and emerged with two.

"You always wondered what's going to happen if they need another goalie," Ruggiero said that night. "If you really think about it, it's better for the organization to have two guys that can potentially practice if they need."

Smith and Ruggiero were on the ice for practice the next day and were treated like members of the team. "You guys sign the fuckin' waiver?" Thornton asked after skating over to them. Ruggiero attended a handful of games the rest of the season with goalie gear waiting in his car, temporarily bringing back hockey's EBUG tradition that dated to the early days of the NHL.

Ruggiero tried to catch on with a team full time and was offered the position as the Detroit Red Wings emergency backup goaltender. But the NHL clarified that EBUGs could not have professional experience, which ruled him out.

"Hockey will break your heart," he said. "You play and you sacrifice a lot, and you see a lot of cool things and you meet people and on the other hand, it's a long road. If anything, there's people in my life that didn't even know me as a hockey player. All of a sudden, these people in my life are like, 'Whoa, we didn't know this about you.'"

Years after trimming his dreadlocks and ditching his beach lifestyle, Ruggiero returned to hockey as a coach and now runs Cat Eye Goaltending camps at Mount Clemens Ice Arena outside Detroit.

Smith became the Predators' emergency backup goaltender and got a close call in 2017 with the Boston Bruins when Tuukka Rask took a puck to the throat. It got so far that Smith was called down to get his gear on just in case anything happened to Bruins replacement Zane McIntyre. Smith got to dress and back up for the Colorado Avalanche on December 16, 2021, against the Predators.

Trying out for Florida didn't get Smith that position, but he looks back fondly on the experience.

"There were a lot of really awesome people, and I got to meet a lot of really great goalies," Smith said.

As negative as the situation was when Luongo and Montoya were injured, nothing but positives came from the "Goal of a Lifetime" promotion. Luukko saw it as an important moment for the organization and Panthers fans. The team missed the playoffs in 12 of the previous 13 seasons and hadn't won a round since an improbable run to the Stanley Cup Final in 1996.

"The franchise has certainly had more downs than ups after a great playoff run early on. It was good that the focus was frankly on the Panthers leaguewide and throughout North America," he said. "To me, it was just another opportunity that something cool was happening in Florida and this franchise wasn't dead, that Vinnie [Viola] bought the franchise and now it was time to move forward. It had a lot of that type of significance."

More than anything, it shifted the focus temporarily away from the debacle of March 3, which the NHL not long after instituted new rules to fix. In South Florida, the tryout brought some levity and fun to a situation that didn't have much when it was happening.

"We're in sports. We're in entertainment here," Luukko said. "We can't always take ourselves too seriously, so it was a fun way to determine it.

"Everybody had a lot of fun. We made such national attention with the game itself when both goalies got hurt, and it just kind of kept the buzz around it—*OK, here's what they're doing to solve it.* It showed a lot of creativity."

CHAPTER 5

THE EQUIPMENT MANAGER: JORGE ALVES' 7.6 UNFORGETTABLE SECONDS

JORGE ALVES had already put his goalie mask back in his locker stall and considered leaving the bench to return to the locker room and take the rest of his gear off to prepare to do his regular job. The Carolina Hurricanes equipment manager, who was dressing as an emergency backup goaltender, was already thinking about his full-time responsibilities as time ticked away in the third period of their game at the Tampa Bay Lightning on December 31, 2016.

The Lightning were up 3–1 in the final moments of a tough loss for the Hurricanes when starting goaltender Cam Ward was summoned to the bench. Alves thought Ward was being pulled for an extra skater. What Alves didn't expect was for coach Bill Peters to call for him to put his gear on and go into the game. After someone retrieved his mask, Alves skated toward the crease and stared up at the clock to see 7.6 seconds left.

It was his first game in uniform, and he was already living a dream just by sitting on the bench in a National Hockey League game. He had no idea he would ever find himself in net.

After spending countless practice sessions taking shots from Hurricanes players and years in a similar role in just about every minor league, Alves wasn't nervous. He also did not think it was a big deal—until it finally sank in.

Oh, shit, I actually got into an NHL game, he thought.

But how, exactly, did Alves get there?

———————

Twin brothers Jorge and Ricardo Alves hated hockey.

Born in 1979 and growing up in a house with one television in Stoughton, Massachusetts, they'd get home from school in the late '80s and early '90s only to find their father, Francisco, a Montreal Canadiens fan, watching hockey.

One day, in middle school, they were at a neighbor's house across the street cleaning out his basement when they found his old lacrosse equipment. That started them on a path not in lacrosse but playing street hockey. "At least we got something to put on our heads now," Jorge thought.

Ricardo played defense. Jorge was inspired to be a goaltender. The brothers did some janitorial shifts at their mother's office, where she made microchips and worked for former Boston Bruins goalie Cleon Daskalakis. Hanging on the wall behind Daskalakis' desk was a large photo of him in full Bruins gear.

"I'd go in there to clean up his office. I'd look up there like, 'Man that's cool. You got all the gear and everything,'" Jorge said. "I was like, 'This is awesome.'"

He started drawing on his street hockey masks and wanted to be like Bruins goalie Andy Moog, whose bear design was one of the NHL's most impressive looks in the early 1990s.

Parents Francisco and Maria were born in Madeira, Portugal, and emigrated to the United States. The family couldn't afford to put Jorge and Ricardo Alves into organized hockey, so they started skating at Asiaf Arena in nearby Brockton, Massachusetts, and got on the ice any way they could after breaking into the sport late as teenagers.

"Our goals were, 'Hey, the middle school has hockey that's free to play,'" Jorge said. "You just have to have the grades. That's free to play, so we're like, 'We're going to play middle school, we're going to play high school,' and the big thing is to get a letter and play varsity hockey."

With actual goaltending equipment, Jorge Alves played and starred for the Black Knights at Stoughton High School. Still, he didn't see an immediate future playing hockey and signed up for a delayed-entry program to join the United States Marine Corps after graduation. Alves didn't know at the time that junior and college teams were asking his high school coach about him but were rebuffed because he was heading to the Marines.

Sure enough, Alves set out for bootcamp. He only learned of the interest in him when he returned home while on leave to find he had been sent letters from junior hockey teams.

"I didn't even know they were interested," he said. "It was one of those things where, you know what, I made a decision to do this and that's fine."

Alves was stationed at Camp Lejeune in North Carolina and in Okinawa, Japan, for six months of jungle warfare training. He remembers the humidity that took the creases out of his neatly pressed and starched camouflage uniform in a matter of minutes—and, of course, the snakes.

"We'd get up at like 4:30 in the morning, still dark out, to do our morning work and we'd be keeping our eyes open for habu snakes," he said. "It was not uncommon for us to come across venomous spiders or dangerous snakes and things like that, and it was just regular. It was just normal."

What wasn't normal or common was hockey, so Alves played soccer in Okinawa and North Carolina. Naturally, he was a goalie there, too.

"It was one of those things, you're just defending the goal no matter what sport it was," he said. "I never liked basketball much because goaltending was illegal."

Alves' four-year tour in the Marines lasted from 1997 to 2001. The time in Japan brought reflection and perspective on what was next. While sitting in a fighting hole in the middle of the woods, he shivered in the cold and thought to himself, *Life is short. I'm not taking it for granted. When I'm done with my term, I'm going after what I want to do in life.*

After returning to the United States, he met his now wife, Amanda, on his 20th birthday—January 30, 1999—after sky-diving with friends in Henderson, North Carolina. The club in which Jorge and Amanda met that night later turned into the Hurricanes' longtime practice rink.

Skating all around the area, Alves was determined to resume his love of hockey.

"I kind of had to put hockey on the back burner for a little while," he said. "And once I got out I was like, 'All right, I'm going to start playing again.'"

While taking evening classes at North Carolina State University, Alves began playing for the school's club hockey team and backstopped the Wolfpack to a conference championship in 2003.

As it turned out, that was just the beginning of his journey.

––––––––––––

The 2004–05 NHL lockout opened a life-changing opportunity for Alves. Carolina's goaltenders were not in town during the summer, so a few players who knew Alves asked if he could skate with them. Rod Brind'Amour, fifteen years into his pro career, was among the players taking shots on him.

Brind'Amour made a career out of his intense workout regimen—"Rod the Bod" was a fitting nickname—and Alves tried to keep up. After four years in the military and some time playing college club hockey, the opportunity to work out with professional players off the ice and take pucks from them on the ice kept him as sharp as ever.

Hanging with the Hurricanes also opened the door for Alves' future as an equipment manager. He met longtime equipment staffer Wally Tatomir and offered to do whatever it took to stay around the team.

"I'd offer up, 'Hey, if you need me to help out and clean up and stuff like that, I'll do that,'" Alves said. "That's what I did. I basically cleaned up at the practice rink afterward."

Playing at NC State and living in Raleigh showed Alves how much hockey had grown around the South.

While skating with the Hurricanes, he heard about free-agent tryout camps in the Southern Professional Hockey League and thought he might have a shot. He made the hour drive south to Fayetteville, North Carolina, to try out for the FireAntz before the 2004–05 season and was blown away by the number of experienced goaltenders he was competing against. In that instance, the NHL lockout wasn't helping him, since so many goalies were without a place to play.

Still, Alves was one of the few left standing by the end of camp. Being a short drive away undoubtedly helped his case. The team told him to stay by his phone and wait for a call. In the meantime, he took part in informal skates with the Hurricanes while the NHL and its players went through negotiations that ended up wiping out the entire 2004–05 season. Alves dressed as an EBUG with the FireAntz a handful of times, and word of his availability began to spread.

By summer 2005, Alves had the title of Hurricanes assistant equipment manager but also wanted to get noticed more as a goaltender. He asked one of Carolina's coaches what he needed to do to be seen and move forward. He was told to shoot for jobs in the East Coast Hockey League, a level up from the Southern Professional Hockey League and two notches below the NHL.

Alves drove five hours to North Charleston, South Carolina, to try out for the ECHL's South Carolina Stingrays. He appeared in preseason games, made an impression on the coaching staff, and was again told to wait for a call. In the ECHL, he was shuffled behind prospects who had been selected in the NHL draft and were often on NHL or American Hockey League contracts.

"That was the good part about me getting my foot in the door in the ECHL, but it was kind of bad because I was always competing with a bunch of guys," Alves said. "I was really there to make sure I could fill in the spot in case they needed it, not so much try to get involved and solidify myself as a starter or something, which I knew was a long shot anyways. It was tough, but at the same time, it was a dream and I wanted to pursue it."

———

Alves kept his equipment in his yellow pickup truck and often wouldn't know how long he'd be spending with any given ECHL team. Some coaches would give him a timeline—a week, maybe a weekend or perhaps a month. Others shed much less light on his situation, which was largely dependent on when another goaltender would be back from injury or be sent down from another minor league.

He would walk into the rink, see another goalie's equipment bag sitting in the locker room, and know his time with a team was up. He then would put his stuff back in the truck and wait for the next call, knowing that he'd take whatever the job was to make sure coaches noticed him.

Alves didn't always wait. If he saw an NHL or AHL goalie had been injured, he'd start making calls to that team's ECHL affiliate to see if it needed a replacement. He had the hierarchy memorized—if the Washington Capitals had an injury, he knew the Hershey Bears would send someone up to the parent club and that the Stingrays might lose someone.

"I kind of learned how to be an agent," he said. "I was always trying to figure stuff out."

Alves got into one game—for a total of four minutes—with the Stingrays during the 2005–06 season. He also spent a lot of time with the ECHL's Greenville Grrrowl, which had goalie prospects from the NHL's Chicago Blackhawks and Edmonton Oilers and little room for outsiders. At any given time, he was one of four goalies in Greenville and became a glorified practice player. He was always healthy, thanks to his workouts with Brind'Amour and a commitment to being available, and that kept Alves under contract.

"They just went ahead and signed me because there was no point in letting me go," Alves said. "They needed me."

Alves got into one game for Greenville, playing 29 minutes and stopping seven of the eight shots he faced. But it wasn't until the next season that he felt needed. He attended training camp in 2006 with the Charlotte Checkers, a team less than a three-hour drive from Raleigh, and was again released at the end of it. He returned to the Hurricanes to help with equipment duties for visiting teams when they were in town, until another ECHL team inquired about him.

One phone call took him back to South Carolina, a place where he was known well as the backup who warmed the bench. During a morning skate on a game day, coach Jared Fitzsimmons approached Alves and asked, "How do you feel about getting traded today?"

"Wait, what?" Alves responded. He knew Capitals prospect Daren Machesney was being traded to the Stingrays, but three teams were interested in trading for him. One was Charlotte, which just happened to be playing at South Carolina that night.

Alves packed up his equipment for the shortest move of many during his career: down the hall from the home locker room to the visiting locker room at the North Charleston Coliseum. He dressed for the Checkers and sat on the other bench, shocking Stingrays fans, who asked what he was doing there. Alves was more than happy to tell them he got traded.

"I think it was for something like money or future considerations," he said. "For all I know, it was a bag of pucks."

At home, Amanda, Alves' wife, asked him why he wasn't getting a chance to play. She was fervently supportive of him chasing his dream. He told her he just had to keep working and be patient. Alves played in two games for a total of 25 minutes with the ECHL's Pensacola Ice Pilots during that 2006–07 season, but he received some clarity one day with South Carolina.

The Stingrays were playing on back-to-back days and starter Davis Parley had faced a heavy workload in the first game. Reporters asked Fitzsimmons why the team didn't just start Alves. It was simple—the developmental goalies were there to play, and they were going to get every single opportunity.

Alves didn't give up, but his priorities changed. He understood no team was trying to turn him into a starter and took pride in staying healthy and being the "break glass in case of emergency" goaltender. From 2004–13, he signed with more than a dozen teams, including the Southern Professional Hockey League's FireAntz, Asheville Aces, Twin City Cyclones, and Knoxville Ice Bears. His hockey career outlasted several of them.

"I think I was involved with three or four teams that ended up folding after the season ended," Alves said. "It took me to 'I have to start all over again' in my search for playing. It is what it is."

Often, players would pull up in a team bus, see Alves' unmistakable yellow pickup truck, and not know if he'd be playing with them or against them. He was perfectly fine with that.

"I realized there's a role here in being the backup and it's not easy. It's not easy to make sure you're in shape. It's not easy to make sure you're healthy to be able to be relied on," Alves said. "I'm the guy that's here for them in case they need me. I'm reliable. The fact is they need a goalie, and they need him right away."

Sometimes a goalie is needed in a matter of hours, which Alves found out on New Year's Eve 2016.

———————

Alves was in his fifth season as the Hurricanes' head equipment manager. He had taken over in summer 2012 when Tatomir retired.

"We're happy that after years as an apprentice and assistant with the equipment staff, Jorge will join us full time," Stanley Cup–winning general manager Jim Rutherford said when Alves earned the promotion. Alves quickly became a beloved and indispensable member of the team by handling equipment responsibilities and serving as a practice goalie.

"Jorgie, he's the man," Hurricanes captain Jordan Staal said. "He shows up every day with a smile on his face and he's ready to work. He's a guy that you can go to for everything and he'll look you straight in the eye and say, 'Yep, no problem,' and he's like that every day. NHL guys can be demanding about little things that might not mean much, but he doesn't really make a stink about anything.

"He's an absolute workaholic. He's there for you every day. He's an absolute treat to be around. He's always in a good mood and ready to do anything for you and would jump on the ice any time you'd ask him to take pucks. And guys have no mercy, but he just takes it and loves it and just loves the game and loves being a goalie."

The Hurricanes won the Stanley Cup in 2006 with Brind'Amour as their captain and rookie Cam Ward in net. Ward and Alves made an immediate connection with some goalie talk, discussing equipment and everything that went into the position.

"A kid that just absolutely loved the game of hockey, was super passionate about the game and trying to be involved," Ward said. "I always kind of joked around that he was like Rudy from the movie, the little guy that just has a huge heart and works his tail off at anything he was doing."

By 2016, Brind'Amour had moved into coaching as an assistant and Ward was in his 12th NHL season. A whole new generation of players began to appreciate Alves' willingness to jump on the ice to help out at practice or a morning skate.

"Any time our goalies needed a break or anybody wanted to go out for extra shots, Jorgie goes out there," longtime Hurricanes executive Don Waddell said. "We knew he had played goal growing up until he got into the equipment side. We felt very comfortable with Jorge and his ability to go in there. We felt if we ever had to play Jorge, we wouldn't have had an issue at all."

The day before the calendar flipped to 2017, the Hurricanes were in Tampa, Florida, the morning after beating the Boston Bruins 3–2 in overtime at home in Raleigh. Ward stopped 31 of the 33 shots he faced in that game, so he figured to get the night off against the Lightning.

Backup Eddie Lack had been out since November 10 because of a concussion and had finally worked his way back into shape to play. A few days before a game that would have been his first in seven weeks, the Swedish goalie started feeling off again but did not say anything.

"I didn't want to complain, so I sucked it up a little bit," Lack said.

After flying with the team to Tampa, Lack skated at Amalie Arena on the morning of December 31.

"I didn't feel as myself and I was like, 'I've got to sit out,'" Lack said. "I just didn't feel right, and I didn't want to put me or my teammates in that position when I was out there and I wasn't feeling good."

Alves was at the rink with Lack, and the two walked back to the team hotel together, laughing and joking around. Alves did not know anything was wrong.

"Everything seemed fine," Alves said.

He was eating his lunch when he got the phone call from assistant general manager Ricky Olczyk. Lack had reported the concussion symptoms to the team. It was the first season of the NHL's enhanced concussion protocol, so everyone was being extra cautious. It became clear that Lack would not be able to play and Ward would have to start for a second consecutive night.

Ordinarily in that situation the Hurricanes would call the Charlotte Checkers, who by then had joined the AHL as their top minor league affiliate, and summon NHL veteran Michael Leighton or prospect Daniel Altshuller. But the Checkers were almost 2,000 miles away in Winnipeg, Manitoba. Even the ECHL's Florida Everblades were on the road—coincidentally, at the South Carolina Stingrays—and could not get a goalie to Tampa in time.

"My first reaction was, 'Is Wardo OK? What's wrong with Wardo? What's wrong with Eddie?'" Alves said. "It was conflicting emotions because I didn't want to see anybody get hurt and obviously it was serious because [Lack] could not dress. A lot of mixed emotions with that."

Tatomir for years told Alves to always have his equipment at the ready. He was talking more about being prepared for the occasional practice or morning skate, but the advice served Alves well. He got ready to dress in an NHL game for the first time as Ward's backup.

"I just knew that I was going to have to start again and that Jorgie was going to be the emergency backup," Ward said. "We always kind of joked that we were waiting for an opportunity like this for him to jump in there."

Ward got a head start before word began to spread among the rest of the Hurricanes' players at their pregame meal.

"We start hearing the rumor that Jorgie's suiting up with us, and we all start getting pumped up just because it's Jorgie and we all love him," defenseman Jaccob Slavin said. "Then we find out it's actually happening. We were so ecstatic for him."

———

Alves signed a professional tryout contract that afternoon, a moment Ward remembers for the smile on Alves' face.

Alves, a month shy of his 38th birthday, put on a white jersey with the No. 40 and his name on it. He put on all his gear and was ready for the chance.

"Seeing him get dressed for warm-ups, seeing the emotion on his face—literally, his dream had come true," Ward said. "We were all stressing about the game and stuff and then you see Jorge who's teary-eyed going out for warm-ups."

Alves joined the Hurricanes in the tunnel for pregame warm-ups and stepped on to the ice. They let him take the traditional solo lap around the ice reserved for rookies making their NHL debut before joining him.

Even during the game, Alves sharpened players' skates and taped up sticks while in uniform.

"Can't shake the habit," Alves said with a smile. "I have a duty to the team."

When he wasn't doing his day job, Alves sat at the end of Carolina's bench and felt like he was living out a dream. Almost every time he worked out with NHL players for more than a decade, he thought about the possibility but knew the chances were slim to nil.

Having been an EBUG so many times in the minors, Alves knew the deal.

"You're an emergency backup," he said. "You're backing up in case there was an emergency. So the only way you're going to play would be if the goalie got hurt—something happened. So when I'm sitting there backing up and they're talking about emergency goalie, this and that, I'm thinking in my head, 'Unless Cam Ward goes down, I'm not going in anyways.'"

Ward did not go down with an injury. Playing his second game in as many days, Ward was solid, but he still allowed three goals on 25 shots—two on the power play in the first period and another in the second. Sebastian Aho scored in the second period to cut Tampa Bay's lead to 3–1, but the Hurricanes couldn't mount a comeback against future Vezina Trophy–winning Lightning goaltender Andrei Vasilevskiy.

Alves' mind was racing midway through the third period, but his thoughts had little to do with the game unfolding before him. He thought about getting the team packed up and all the bags out of the arena and onto the bus and to the airport for the flight home. He left his mask in the locker room to give himself a head start because as soon as the final horn went off, Alves was ready to race back to pack up his own stuff before helping his staff load up the rest of the Hurricanes' equipment.

"I wasn't thinking about anything else," he said.

Alves sat on the bench appreciating the experience. Out of all the goalies he had backed up in the minors, how many got to put on an NHL uniform for even one game? He considered it an amazing, once-in-a-lifetime experience. Little did Alves know that Peters, the coach, was contemplating trying to find a time to get him on the ice.

That time came with a whistle with 7.6 seconds left in the third period. Peters called Ward to the bench, and Alves thought the move was to get an extra skater on the ice.

"You cool with putting in Jorge?" Peters asked. Ward responded, "Absolutely. Get him in there."

Peters peered around Ward to Alves, who was waiting in the tunnel. Peters told Alves to put his gear on and get into the game. Ward saw excitement but mostly surprise in Alves' eyes and gave him a little encouragement.

"I was like, 'No, seriously, go get your helmet on,'" Ward said. "You kind of had to tell him twice, 'No, we're not playing. Get out there.'"

Fellow equipment manager Bob Gorman sprinted to the locker room to retrieve Alves' mask. Alves stepped on the ice and waited for Gorman to return with his mask.

He slipped it on, and referee Eric Furlatt gave Alves a tap on the backside and told him, "Hurry up and get in there." Alves apologized and collected himself.

While public address announcer Paul Porter introduced him to the crowd as Carolina's new goaltender, Alves wondered how many people were thinking, *Who is Jorge Alves and what is going on right now?* But he had a job to do. Mask on, he hustled to the crease, held on to the crossbar, and tapped the right post, then the left, and made sure his equipment was secured just right.

"Most of the time, goalies get thrown in, they'll get down and start stretching out," he said. "I remember telling myself, 'Don't stretch.'"

As Peters took a sip of water on the bench, Alves settled into the net and looked up at the clock and back down to the ice.

"To actually get out there, all of a sudden the lights seemed brighter," Alves said. "Seeing 7.6 seconds, it's an image I'll never forget. Just looking up there and seeing time on the board and me on the ice."

Staal and the Hurricanes couldn't contain their excitement on the bench.

"I was just overjoyed seeing him out there. I thought that was so cool," Staal said. "Seeing him step on the ice was a pretty cool moment. I know it was special for him, but it was just really cool to see and just knowing how he is [as a person] made it all that much better."

The puck was dropped 180 feet away, at the other end of the rink to Vasilevskiy's right. Temporary teammate Brock McGinn lost the game's final faceoff to Tampa Bay's Valtteri Filppula and the Lightning ran out the clock in their own zone. Alves joked afterward that he looked at the puck in the far corner and said to himself, "Stay in that corner." But really, he would have loved some action.

"It's not like I felt like they were going to come down on a breakaway or anything," Alves said. "I just kind of knew it was going to get stuck down in that corner and I'm like, 'Welp, just let it go.' I really did wish. In a perfect world, I'm like, 'Maybe there was enough time for their guy to come on a breakaway and me just make a huge save at the last second,' but that didn't work out," Alves said.

———————

Alves skated off the ice with the record of the shortest debut for a goaltender in NHL history.

"It was unbelievable," said Waddell, who was Carolina's team president at the time. "It might only be eight seconds, but he got that chance to put that jersey on and actually play in net. It's another thing that he'll never forget and we won't forget as a franchise."

Instead of racing to get the Hurricanes packed up, Alves was the guest of honor in the locker room after a game that didn't go their way. Still, it didn't feel like a loss because of their equipment manager's 7.6 seconds of fame.

"In the room, we were so happy for him. It was something he would have never dreamt could have come true," Slavin said. "I don't know if that guy ever walks in the locker room because he's always running to do the next thing for somebody who asked him to do it. It's been unbelievable just to be able to work with him, and then the guys knowing how passionate Jorge is, about not only the Canes but just hockey in general, it was so cool to see it for him and see him live out a dream that he probably never thought was possible."

Brind'Amour, who went back with Alves to their practice skates in summer 2004, could feel the joy from the coaches' room.

"You have a lifetime employee that's the hardest-working guy in the organization—and everybody knows it in the organization,"

Brind'Amour said. "But nobody knows who he is outside the organization. If there's ever a guy that deserves some credit, that's the guy. That's why everyone felt so great about it—just the fact that he could get in there. Because he literally is a jack-of-all-trades in the hockey business."

Lack, who got to know Alves well from so much time together on and off the ice, said, "It couldn't happen to a better guy than him."

With 7.6 seconds of NHL action, Alves had reached the NHL. After figuring he'd get chirped by players and friends for what could only be considered a sip of coffee in the world's best hockey league, he realized through countless interviews and requests how big of a deal it was around the sport.

"I didn't really do anything on the ice," he said. "I'm like, 'This is crazy.'"

What was even crazier was trying to play recreational hockey in the aftermath of the shortest career in NHL history. In summer 2017, a buddy invited Alves to play in USA Hockey's adult league national tournament, which happened to be taking place that year in Tampa. After agreeing, Alves was told officials weren't going to let him participate because he played in the NHL the previous season.

The team had other former NHL players who were allowed to skate because their careers had been over for some time. Alves worked the phones.

"After a few phone calls explaining the scenario, 'Here's the situation,' I ended up getting to play," he said. "But it was weird having that actually be an issue."

And then there was the mail. Alves started getting packages sent to his house: pictures from the game or Upper Deck's "Young Guns" card the company made for him to sign and send back. Five years later, he was still getting mail.

He is still the head equipment manager and practices with the Hurricanes, on occasion, though much has changed personally from his early days.

"He's a great human being, a great dad," Brind'Amour said. "You can't ask for more out of that guy."

Alves' daughter, Madison, was born in 2007, and his son, Jaxon, was born three years later. He and Amanda put them in skates and on the ice at age three, but neither got into hockey immediately. As much as Alves is the hero of every goalie who toils in the minors waiting for the opportunity to make it to the NHL, even for a day, he tells his children at older ages now that they can still lace up skates and give it a try given how late he started.

"At your age, I couldn't even skate," Alves has told them. "You guys have fun. Don't feel like you can't pursue it because you're a little bit older. You're nowhere near as old as I was when I started. If you still want to play, there's nothing stopping you. You don't have to start at three years old. You can play whenever you want."

CHAPTER 6

THE ACCOUNTANT: SCOTT FOSTER'S 14 MINUTES OF FAME

SCOTT FOSTER saw a jersey with his name on it hanging in the Chicago Blackhawks locker room and made the decision right away—he would put on all his goaltending gear, so he could slip on the jersey on top.

The 36-year-old accountant who played hockey in a couple of beer leagues figured this was the best it could possibly get, so he wasn't doing anything halfway. Foster dressed like he was in the National Hockey League, sat with Blackhawks players in their lounge at United Center, and watched the game happening on the ice against the Winnipeg Jets.

Foster had done the emergency backup goaltender thing more than a dozen times already that season, but on March 29, 2018, he had to be ready at a moment's notice because the Blackhawks only had one healthy goalie in uniform. When Collin Delia went down after making a save almost six minutes into the third period and had to be helped off the ice, Foster froze. He didn't hear the equipment manager telling him to grab his mask, blocker, and gloves and get ready to go in the game.

"You have to get your stuff," he was told a second time. "He is coming out."

For good measure, assistant coach Kevin Dineen left the bench to deliver the same message. Still, Foster had no words. He gathered his stuff, picked out the goalie stick he thought had more life left in it, and began the walk to the ice and the record books as the first EBUG in modern history to enter an NHL game.

Foster cried the first time he put on skates and the rest of his hockey equipment. He cried so much that his parents, Greg and Christine, told him he would not have to go back. So, naturally, he cried about that, too, because he didn't want to give it up. Just like for most kids across Canada, hockey was the sport to take up in the winter at an early age. It was the 1980s, Wayne Gretzky was in his prime playing for the Edmonton Oilers, and the love of the sport was certainly alive for Scott growing up in Sarnia, Ontario.

But Foster from the start didn't seem like he wanted to be like Gretzky. More like Grant Fuhr, or specifically one of the Toronto Maple Leafs' goaltenders in those days, Allan Bester. He held his tiny hockey stick like a goalie, halfway down, and acted like one as soon as the games began.

"I'm just going into the net trying to block shots in player equipment," Foster said. "It just seemed like I was drawn to the position early on."

He had an older cousin who was a goaltender, and it just felt natural. By the time he started playing organized hockey at age six, Foster took his turn in goal, pitched a shutout, and decided the net was the place for him. It was the first shutout of his life but certainly not his last or most memorable. The first photo of young Scott in goalie gear also foreshadowed his future—he was wearing a Point Edward Blackhawks jersey.

Foster played Single A and Double A hockey because that's what was available to kids in the Sarnia area of Southern Ontario, across the Canada–U.S. border from Port Huron, Michigan. He was in his early teenage years in the mid-1990s by the time he played Peewee hockey at the Triple A level around Lambton County. At that point, he was reliant on his parents to drive him to games and practices wherever he and his team could get on the ice.

He was one year younger than Petrolia, Ontario, native and budding goalie prospect Michael Leighton, who went on to get drafted by the Blackhawks, play 127 NHL games, and set the American Hockey League shutout record. Foster didn't get that kind of attention, but he held his own.

"I don't know if I was always the most flashy one or anything like that," Foster said. "I guess I just did my thing."

Like every aspiring player at that age, Foster set the goal of playing junior hockey. When he was a late cut from a team at 16 and couldn't land a spot elsewhere, he went back to playing Single A midget hockey. It was a huge blow to his confidence.

"I just assumed I was playing junior at that point," he said, "and now I wasn't."

It turned out to be one of the most critical years of Foster's career. A coaching change with the team he was cut from months earlier opened a door. The new coach was letting one of the team's goalies go and invited Foster to practice and play games. After worrying about not having any hockey to play at the start of the season, he was in two leagues and often on the ice twice a day. Foster played 10 or 12 games at the Tier 2 junior level, then played Tier 3 for the Mooretown Flags in 1999–2000. Camp in Sarnia brought more uncertainty for Foster, who was told to hang around and asked the team to sign him or trade him. The Petrolia Jets of the Greater Ontario Hockey League acquired his rights, and he went to play for them under his old coach in 2000.

"It kind of links back to that one year where I thought it was kind of all done," he said. "It turned out to be where a lot of connections were made and growth in my game and such that I landed where I needed to be to kind of make that next step in my career."

———

Foster always assumed growing up he'd play at the major junior level in the Ontario Hockey League, but it was clear by age 18 that wasn't going to happen, so he set his focus on playing college hockey in the U.S.

"That's what you thought the progression was, not college hockey," he said. "It wasn't on my radar until later when you realized just because you missed the OHL boat, there's another boat to catch, which ultimately was probably the more important boat in terms of life outside of hockey."

Foster had a 2.27 goals-against average and .928 save percentage for Petrolia in 2000–01. By that point, his game had rounded out and he was getting attention from U.S. schools with strong programs looking to bring him in. He was invited to play Division I hockey at Ferris State University in Michigan but wasn't ready to make that leap.

"I never had been to the school," he said. "I didn't know anything about it. It would have kind of been blind faith."

Foster decided instead to return to Petrolia for a second season in 2001. Western Michigan University was interested, and he got a chance to visit the campus in Kalamazoo before committing in the fall. Senior goalie Jeff Reynaert was moving on after the season, and there was a chance for Foster to play for the Broncos right away. It felt like a good fit, plus Foster was offered the scholarship while playing a road game for the Jets in his hometown of Sarnia.

"Kind of full-circle there," he said.

Foster was able to take in a game at Western Michigan a few months later in January 2002. Michigan State was in town with goalie Ryan Miller, who was by then a blue-chip NHL prospect on the verge of joining the Buffalo Sabres. Reynaert stopped all 24 shots he faced, Western Michigan won the game 2–0, and Foster was able to see how fun an atmosphere it could be.

"I knew at that point I made absolutely the right decision," he said. "It was just too much fun. I couldn't imagine even really playing elsewhere."

Foster was not sure what he wanted to do for a career outside hockey. His top priority was getting on the ice and playing. He figured he'd enroll somewhere that had a business school, and Western Michigan checked that box.

Two weeks into his freshman year in the fall of 2002, he met Erin Komasinski, an Indiana native who was on the women's track and field team. Foster remembers he "struck out immensely" the first time he tried to date her, then he unjammed some quarters in the laundry machine and they began seeing each other. Seven years later, they got married.

"I don't think she had even been on skates until she met me, and now she was attending college hockey games and had access to the rink to go on the ice," he said. "She got dragged right into the hockey world quickly. I don't know if she bargained for many, many years later what it would ultimately mean."

On the ice, Foster got every opportunity to play that he had hoped for. He started his first college game as a freshman and played 21 in total. He finished with a 3.77 goals-against average and .868 save percentage. Western Michigan struggled as a team that season, going 15–21–2.

"It was good and bad at times," he said. "The adjustment was tough. We just ultimately didn't have results."

Foster played even more his sophomore year, getting into the net 33 times as Western Michigan's No. 1 goaltender. His numbers improved a bit to a 3.24 goals-against average and .881 save percentage, and the Broncos won 17 of their 39 games. Foster's third year in college was tough because coach Jim Culhane and his staff turned the goaltending duties over to freshman Daniel Bellissimo as the starter and sophomore Eric Marvin the backup. Foster was frozen out of any game action that season.

"I'm not saying that I was a world-beater in college, but at some point you figured there was a shake-up made because they weren't happy with the results when you were playing," he said. "Why are you not getting a chance to win a game or something? Those were coaches' decisions that were made."

Foster went into the summer of 2005 knowing he couldn't change Culhane's mind, so he was determined to control what he could and enjoy the playing time he got. He attended the camp run by renowned NHL goaltending coach Mitch Korn, who had helped Dominik Hasek become one of hockey's best netminders with Buffalo in the 1990s and was six years into his job with the Nashville Predators.

"I don't know if it was as much for the on-ice stuff as it was for kind of the off-ice and the mental side of the game and just sort of the reset that it provided me—how to approach the game and some of that mental skill side of it," he said. "I think it was a really good summer for me."

That good summer turned into a cruel fall for Foster, who got to play the third period of Western Michigan's exhibition against

Brock University on October 8 and then again a week later in the regular season opener against Robert Morris. Foster allowed three goals—two on the power play and one short-handed—on seven shots in the final 20 minutes of a 5–2 loss in front of a crowd of 2,520.

"I don't know that I remember playing poorly, but it also wasn't probably my best," he said. "It's results that count, right? And that was the last sniff I got. Sort of a disappointing end."

It was the last game of Foster's college career and what he thought was his final taste of competitive hockey.

———

Foster held no grudges against Bellissimo and was valued enough inside the Western Michigan men's hockey program that he was offered a graduate student position for 2006–07. He had completed his undergraduate degree in accounting and was working on a master's in accountancy.

"The classes just kind of clicked," he said of his focus on accounting. "It was something that I understood. I'm not saying that it came easy, but it wasn't something that I struggled with."

Erin accepted a job at an architecture firm in Chicago that she had interned for during college, so she moved there while Scott wrapped up grad school. While working on his master's, the graduate assistant gig allowed him to do some video work and other tasks to stay in hockey. It also gave him his first close call as an emergency backup goaltender.

Foster was in his apartment when he got a call that the American Hockey League's Grand Rapids Griffins needed a goalie for at least their morning skate before facing the Toronto Marlies. Former college teammate Jeff Campbell played for the Griffins, and the hour drive from Kalamazoo was easy enough.

Foster was on the ice for the morning skate, the Detroit Red Wings were able to get another goalie to Grand Rapids on time to help their top farm team out, and Foster didn't even get as close as putting on a Griffins jersey that night.

"I just went home, back to school," he said.

With his master's degree complete, Scott joined Erin in Chicago and began working on mutual funds as a staff accountant. His first job lasted two years until his entire department was eliminated, and he spent six years at his next stop before joining Golub Capital in 2016.

They were married in 2009 and Erin gave birth to the couple's first daughter, Morgan, in 2013. Scott got into a routine of playing hockey in two beer leagues at Johnny's IceHouse, which also doubled as the Blackhawks' practice facility.

Beginning with the 2015–16 season, the NHL had each team come up with a list of local goaltenders who might be available on an emergency basis. The Blackhawks called Johnny's IceHouse owner Tom Moro, and he gave them Foster's name.

Erin was pregnant with their second daughter, Wynnifred, and she and Scott were out celebrating their sixth anniversary with dinner and a movie in the city when he got the email. Ordinarily, he would have put the phone away, but it was from the Blackhawks, so he read it in the movie theater. Foster responded saying he was in and sent the team his information.

"It could be a list of 20 guys for all I knew at that point in time," he said. "It was a funny story, really, to tell people."

Being on the list did not mean much until 2017, when each team was required to have an emergency backup goaltender on site for games. Now it was a time commitment that would have been one more thing to schedule on top of work, family life, and beer league hockey, so Foster's initial reaction was to pull himself from consideration.

"You're a liar. You want to do this," Erin told him. "You're going to do this because you know you want to go to the games."

Scott agreed, and while killing time on a lunch hour in September 2017 selected 12 of the Blackhawks' 41 home games. One of them just happened to be March 29 against the Winnipeg Jets.

Foster thinks he got some top choices because he had a connection to Blackhawks executive assistant Meghan Hunter, who was putting the schedule together. Hunter grew up in Petrolia, Ontario, where Foster played his junior hockey, before moving on to her playing days in Wisconsin and a career in coaching and management.

Foster picked up a few extra games during the 2017–18 season when other EBUGs couldn't make it and had a nice routine. He rode his bike with his daughters in tow to drop them off at school, locked the bike up at the closest Chicago Transit Authority station, and took the train into the city to his office not far from the Willis Tower. He did the reverse trip on the way back and drove to United Center when it was his game night.

Foster had one day early in the 2017–18 season he thought he might get into uniform for a game. It was Sunday, November 5, and the Montreal Canadiens were in town after playing in Winnipeg the previous night. Starter Carey Price was already out with an injury, and they didn't know if Al Montoya, who faced the Jets, would be healthy enough to back up Charlie Lindgren.

Foster was running around a track at the YMCA in Oak Park, Illinois, when someone from the Blackhawks called to tell him the Canadiens might need a goalie. Foster wasn't scheduled to be the emergency backup that night but agreed to take Montreal's call. He had to go in the pool for kiddie swim lessons with Wynnifred and told Erin, "If any number calls this phone, pick it up."

"All of a sudden you're bobbing your daughter in the pool and [Erin is] waving her arms from up above," Foster recalled. "She's like, 'You've got to go tonight. Montreal needs a goalie.'

So I'm like, 'I'm going to go from swimming in a YMCA pool to dressing in an NHL game. That's really something.'"

He got to the game only to find out the Canadiens cleared Montoya to dress. Foster sat next to the scheduled emergency backup goalie in the press box, watched the game, and went home. He figured that's what he signed up for and the closest he'd ever come.

"I thought the closest I'd get to this was going downstairs and putting my gear on," he said. "Never be seen, but it's a cool tale. You're in your gear, maybe getting a sweater with your name if you're lucky, a couple rolls of tape. I don't know."

Foster kept taking his turn going to games. He parked at the loading dock, took the elevator up to the press box, used the second intermission media meal as his dinner, ate a cup of Peanut M&Ms, and watched the game before returning to his car and driving home.

"No expectations," he said. "Never once thinking about going in the game."

Foster was certainly not thinking much about the game on Thursday, March 29, 2018, either.

———

It was late in a lost season for the Chicago Blackhawks, who had lost 46 of their first 77 games. After a nine-year streak of making the playoffs and a run that included three Stanley Cup titles, they were eliminated from postseason contention on March 20. It was too early to say they were rebuilding, but injuries to top goaltender Corey Crawford and others derailed their season and they were sellers at the trade deadline.

"The season had been just OK," first-year assistant Kevin Dineen said.

Captain Jonathan Toews had joined the list of injured Blackhawks players and the game had no meaning for them in the standings. Still, there were some things to celebrate. It was longtime defenseman Brent Seabrook's 1,000th game, plus forward Dylan Sikura was set to make his NHL debut.

While the Blackhawks were on their way down from their contending years, the Winnipeg Jets were on the ascent. They acquired center Paul Stastny and defenseman Joe Morrow at the deadline and cruised into Chicago on a six-game winning streak. Only three teams in the league had more points than Winnipeg's 104—double the Blackhawks' total for the season.

With Crawford out, Anton Forsberg was expected to start in net for Chicago. Prospect Collin Delia, recalled from Rockford of the AHL, was set to back up. It was a busy morning skate for Delia.

"[Goaltending coach Jimmy Waite] would do some goalie work, and afterward I would do some shooting drills with the forwards," Dineen said. "Dells had been called up and was more than willing to take whatever the guys were going to do. We did a shootout and then they played the two-pass game and we had all kinds of stuff going on, and he was all in. He was just doing everything. And, sure enough eight, 10 hours later it kind of bit him in the bum."

Delia might have taken it easier if the team knew he was going to start and make his NHL debut that night. Or if Forsberg's injury had taken place before 5 PM, the Blackhawks could have brought up J-F Berube or Jeff Glass from the IceHogs and likely gotten one of them to the arena on time for puck drop.

But Forsberg was hurt during the Blackhawks' pregame soccer, and it was not minor. The injury actually knocked him out for the remainder of the season. Team officials weren't in desperation mode yet because they had Delia there to play, but the sense of urgency was turned up in the hour before the game.

Head equipment manager Troy Parchman acknowledged afterward he and his staff should have been more prepared for this possibility after their situation in Philadelphia in December 2016. Crawford had appendicitis and underwent an appendectomy the morning of the game, so the Blackhawks contacted the Flyers to get someone from their list of emergency goaltenders and signed 23-year-old Eric Semborski to back up Scott Darling.

That experience was far from Parchman's mind at the start of warm-ups at 7 PM for the 7:30 game against the Jets and he raced to the loading dock to ask Frankie the parking attendant if the emergency backup goalie had arrived yet. No, he hadn't, so Parchman told Frankie to make sure that when the EBUG arrived he was sent directly to the locker room. Parchman set off to find a nameplate, but equipment assistant D.J Kogut had already stitched FOSTER 90 onto a red Chicago home jersey.

"It made it look like we were organized and prepared for it, but we really weren't," Parchman said at the annual Blackhawks convention that summer.

Foster wasn't far away. He had ridden his bike home from the train station, where he and Erin had an argument "about nothing," he said. "Stupid things." He grabbed his gear and began the drive from their house in Oak Park to United Center. It was always his goal to get to the arena by the start of warm-ups.

He was exiting the Eisenhower Expressway on to Damen Avenue when his phone started to buzz with calls and messages asking, "Where are you?" For the first time that day, Foster knew something was off. When he arrived, those suspicions were confirmed. Frankie was more urgent than the previous 14 times Foster parked his car there. Foster was asked to confirm the spelling of his last name, and Frankie grabbed his gear and put it on a cart to be hauled to the locker room.

Foster was guided through the arena and brought up to speed on the situation. Parchman said when he first met Foster, "I tried to be composed, but really I was panicking inside."

"That makes two of us," Foster said later.

The Blackhawks knew Forsberg couldn't dress and that Delia was starting, but they still had a couple of outstanding questions. Should Foster get dressed and try to join the team on the ice for warm-ups? Should he sign a one-day contract that would bind him to the Blackhawks?

"There was some wavering from them," Foster said about the contract. "The moment you sign that for the night, you're the Hawks' guy. And theoretically speaking, the Jets could've went down two guys and you go there."

Foster signed the contract, an amateur tryout agreement that paid him nothing. He was asked if he wanted to go into the weight room to stretch and warm up.

"No, I'm good," he said. "Where is my gear? I'll put my gear on. I'm used to a three-minute warm-up now."

That was when Foster saw the No. 90 jersey with his name on it hanging with all his gear in a locker stall.

"You try not to think about the number choice made for you," he said. "You don't get greedy at that point. You just accept that. But you're in an NHL dressing room putting on a sweater with your name on it that's yours. Your gear's already all hung up nice. It's like you're part of the team. You're in the NHL."

Once the surreal feeling passed, Foster settled in and tried to stay out of the way. His temporary teammates all made a point of approaching him to introduce themselves. The home locker room at United Center was a bit nicer than his usual dressing quarters at Johnny's IceHouse, but it was still "a room full of hockey guys, so you can fit in."

Before the game got underway, Parchman told Foster the team had a flight to catch afterward, so things would go quickly.

"There will be people around," Parchman said. "If you need anything, just ask. You can keep the sweater and you can keep the socks."

Foster then made the decision that would save him valuable minutes later in the night. He strapped on all his gear, from his skates and black leg pads to his chest protector. He was told the team made the call for him not to sit on the bench during the game, which would have prevented him from getting any warm-up shots should he have to enter. He was directed to watch from the players' lounge, so Foster slipped his cell phone into one of the pads in his chest protector, "like any logical person would do," and hobbled carefully from the locker room to the lounge, making sure not to step on any floor tiles with his skate blades.

Already there were the night's scratches, including Toews and Crawford.

"He already won," Dineen said. "It was already the greatest night. You get to watch an NHL game, the Blackhawks, sitting between Toews and Crawford. How good is that? You can't get much better than that."

The longtime NHL veterans thought it was amusing that Foster stood up—in full gear—for the Canadian and U.S. anthems. Then they all watched the pregame ceremony honoring Seabrook for playing in his 1,000th game. With no playoffs on the horizon, 22,000 fans packed United Center that night because of Seabrook more than anything else.

A big spread of food was available in the lounge, and Foster was offered something to eat. He hadn't eaten anything since lunch since he was expecting his usual second intermission dinner in the press box, but he was already in full uniform and wasn't about to risk it.

Foster and the players exchanged some small talk and watched the game.

"There's nothing overly memorable about any conversation," he said. "There's nothing overly shocking about what's taking place."

On the ice, the game was unfolding in shocking fashion. After Delia made a save on Winnipeg's Mark Scheifele with some help from Brandon Saad 43 seconds in, he denied Jets defenseman Dustin Byfuglien among a flurry of early stops. Then Patrick Kane put a perfect shot past goalie Eric Comrie for an unassisted goal to give Chicago a 1–0 lead 3:44 in.

While Delia was busy stopping all 14 Winnipeg shots he faced in the first period, Saad scored to make it 2–0 before intermission. Two goals by Tomas Jurco staked the Blackhawks to a 4–0 lead just over halfway through the game before the Jets finally cracked Delia on Bryan Little's goal 14:24 into the second. Sikura registered his first NHL point by assisting on Erik Gustafsson's goal that gave Chicago some breathing room at 5–1, and Scheifele cut it to 5–2 before the period was over.

It was in the locker room during the second intermission that Foster realized later he should have known something was up. Delia was getting more attention from the training staff.

"Huh, that's weird," Foster thought to himself before letting it slip out of his mind.

Sikura picked up his second NHL point, setting up Alex DeBrincat for an insurance goal 2:11 into the third that made it 6–2 Blackhawks. With just over 14 minutes left, Delia made a seemingly innocuous but impressive save on Winnipeg's Brandon Tanev on a one-timer from 10 feet away.

"Nice save by Delia!" Blackhawks play-by-play announcer Pat Foley said on the home broadcast.

Back in the lounge, players thought Tanev's shot stung Delia in the groin and that he'd need a few seconds to collect himself. But Delia crumpled to the ice and was in obvious distress. Defenseman Jan Rutta bent over to check on the injured goalie, and Blackhawks players called for head athletic trainer Mike Gapski. Delia tried to get to his feet but went right back down in the crease.

Foster, watching on television from the players' lounge, instantly made the connection to the second intermission attention Delia was receiving. Delia was dealing with major cramping problems and had to be helped to his feet by referee Dan O'Rourke, who guided him down the ice with Gapski until forward David Kampf took over.

"Every team playing a home game has to have a third goalie available, and he's going to come in," Foley said as Delia was led off the ice and down the tunnel. "Scott Foster's going to have to come into the game!"

Foster's parents were in town only because it was Easter weekend and only had the game on at his house because he was dressing. They knew their son was going into an NHL game before it sank in for him.

"Your heart rate, it's just like someone floored a gas pedal," Foster said. "But at that point, I am just interpreting what I'm seeing on a TV. I don't have anybody telling me, 'You're going out.'"

Even when he did, Foster didn't get the message. The first time he was told to get his stuff, Foster recalled, "It didn't register." While Toews was going crazy, unbeknownst to him, Foster was told once more it was time to collect his gear because he was going in.

"I don't think I heard anything other than, 'Put your helmet on,'" Foster said afterward.

Blackhawks coaches waiting on the bench had radio contact with Waite and video coach Matt Meacham but not to the locker room, so Dineen left to figure out what was going on.

"He was silent, completely silent," Dineen said. "He didn't have a word to say. He got up and he started getting dressed and he never said anything. I was like, 'I don't even know if he's all right.'"

Dineen went back to the bench, but coach Joel Quenneville wanted to know how much longer until Foster would be ready. Foster didn't need to suit up since he did so before the game started, but Dineen returned and asked how he was doing. Still no response.

While Foster quietly got his stuff together, Dineen told him, "I've played like 1,200 NHL games and I'd give my left nut to be in your situation right now."

"All right, let's go," Foster said.

Before Foster took his final couple of steps down the tunnel toward the bench, Parchman brought him the two sticks he had waiting, each one from back in his Western Michigan days. Foster chose one, but not his usual stick he had been playing beer league games with. Filled with indecision, he called Parchman back and debated in his head before sticking with his first choice.

"For some reason I remembered the other one was on its way out," Foster said. "I'm like, 'I think this one's got more life left in it.'"

Foster shuffled on to the bench and onto the ice for the unlikeliest of NHL debuts.

While Foster was skating toward the Blackhawks net, Dineen whispered to Quenneville, "You've got to take a look at his stick."

"He comes out and he's got a wood goalie stick," Dineen said. "When's the last time you saw a wood goalie stick?"

A handful of thoughts crossed Foster's mind in the few seconds from the bench to the crease—one in particular.

"Yeah, skate sharpening is due. That's not great," Foster thought to himself. "That was scheduled for my next game at Johnny's in a couple days or whatever and I put it off and now I'm in the NHL, so that would've been good to do."

Watching up in the press box, Waite looked over at nearby fans who wanted to know what was going on. "I don't know that guy, either," he said. Only later did Waite find out that Foster usually sits not too far from him during his games.

A half-dozen pucks were thrown out on the ice so Foster could get the warm-up shots he was allowed because he was not on the bench. Defenseman Jordan Oesterle and forward Vinnie Hinostroza alternated shots, but Foster was only looking one way, so six of the 12 shots went in.

"The pucks are going in the net," Foster recalled. "You see one, you make a save, the next one's in the net. Like, this looks great."

Officials were not rushing Foster, who was allowed ample time to get ready because of the emergency nature of the situation. After 12 shots of warm-up, Oesterle and Hinostroza asked Foster if he wanted any more.

"No," he replied. "Let's just go."

There was 14:01 left in the third period. The Blackhawks had a 6–2 lead, but there was no telling how the rest of the game would go. It was the first time in the modern era that an emergency backup goaltender was forced into an NHL game by injury.

"You get to the show, it don't matter how," said Blackhawks color analyst Eddie Olczyk, who played 1,088 NHL games.

The faceoff was to Foster's left, and it was game on. More than 11 years removed from his last competitive hockey game, he zoned out the crowd and turned on his goalie instincts he started developing as a kid in Point Edward, Ontario, and relied on for countless beer league games at Johnny's IceHouse over much of the past decade.

Stop the first shot, Foster thought to himself. *Got to stop the first shot because it's up or down from there.*

Exactly a minute in, 6'8" Jets defenseman Tyler Myers directed the puck on net from the bottom of the faceoff circle to Foster's left. With textbook form, Foster was in the perfect spot for the shot to hit him on the left pad and bounce harmlessly behind the net. The crowd roared in approval.

"Luckily, you get a low percentage wrister from the corner that you get in front of, and that was the moment where it became hockey," Foster said. "It can go very much awry, and I've had lots of games that I've been very prepared to play in go awry. But at least it was that moment to just think, 'That's a save. Just play. And it's going to go how it's going to go, but just play.'"

———————

Tom Fenton got the message from one of his old hockey buddies that "Fozzy" was in the game in Chicago. Then his phone filled up with messages. They grew up together in Sarnia and played junior hockey on the same team. Six-plus years after Fenton backed up one game for the Coyotes, Foster went a step further.

"I was so happy to see him have that experience," Fenton said. "The only bummer part was that was my story to tell, and he one-upped it by actually getting to play."

Fenton was glued to his television from that point on. Of course, he wasn't the only one. A former coworker of Foster's considered himself a casual Blackhawks fan more likely to watch when they're winning a game, so he turned it on with Chicago up four goals. He stood up, took a slow walk toward the TV, waited for the close-up of Foster, and said to his wife, "I know him!"

The hockey community would soon come to know all about Foster.

During one of the first stoppages in play, Foster squirted water into his mouth—from Delia's bottle. It didn't matter that he had only played a couple of minutes, but Foster's big mistake came when his eyes drifted up from the ice to the 300 level at the massive "Madhouse on Madison." He knew the place was full to celebrate Seabrook and for a moment his brain went in slow motion.

"You feel like you're staring in people's eyes, and that was like the perfect reminder of, 'Never look in the stands again for the rest of this time,'" Foster said. "Just don't do it."

Foster had to stay focused. Trailing by four goals in the middle of a playoff race and facing a goalie who wasn't an NHL player, the Jets were thinking about shooting early and often. Kane could feel Winnipeg's desire to shoot, even if it meant firing the puck high and wide.

"Nothing against the goalie, but you want to get as many shots as you can on him and test him early," Little said. "Any goalie coming in in the third period is going to be cold, so you want to get shots. For us, we were trying to force it maybe a little too much."

Foster vividly remembers pockets of time from the night but no actual game play. There was O'Rourke skating behind the net and saying to him, "How 'bout this?" "Yeah, how *'bout* this?" he replied. And then there was the fear of the ice crew shoveling snow that terrified Foster more than taking 90-mph slap shots.

"I was like, 'Where can I stand and not get hit?'" Foster said. "And I'm like, 'I don't know that spot.' That was the moment of, 'I think I'm just going to cause a problem here, so just don't. Just try to get out of the way and let them do their thing.'"

The commercial breaks felt like an eternity for someone accustomed to fast-moving 15-minute periods of beer league hockey. Plenty of goalies go over to the bench for a towel and a quick chat, but Foster couldn't bring himself to do it.

"That would mean conversation," he said. "I would have had to talk to someone on that bench. I wanted no part of it. It's weird those decision points that I made—a second looking at the crowd; don't do that. Don't get hit by a shovel from the ice crew. Don't go to the bench and talk to people."

Foster was in his element in the crease with his eyes locked on the play. He had done this countless times, even if no one was watching.

His second save on Finnish goal-scoring phenom Patrik Laine became a subject of debate with his father back home. Greg Foster joked that he didn't think his son should get credit for the save because Laine missed the net.

"I'm like, 'I got a piece of it,'" Foster said. "'Dad, I'm 36 years old, and I just played an NHL game.'"

Foster's family members were far from the only ones tuning into the game. TSN analyst and longtime NHL forward Ray Ferraro got a sense of the buzz when he checked his phone midway through the third period.

"The word got out that this guy who hasn't played in 15 years is playing goal for the Blackhawks," Ferraro said on the air. "What an amazing night."

The word had reached Johnny's IceHouse a few blocks down the street. One of Foster's two teams was playing in a game he knew he'd be missing to serve as the EBUG for the Blackhawks.

Once the players caught wind that Foster was in for Chicago, they stopped the game. Players and referees in full equipment stood in the Stanley Lounge and watched Foster's appearance on television. Fortunately for them, he kept putting on a show.

Foster got his left skate on Andrew Copp's backhander at the side of the net for his third save, then marveled at Blackhawks players laying out to block shots they ordinarily wouldn't sacrifice their bodies to get in front of.

"They're taking a full extra step to lay out when maybe if it's an NHL goalie in net, he's making the save [and they're thinking], 'I don't need to do it here,'" Foster said. "People want to spin it like they don't trust you. To me that is a sign of respect."

Dineen called it "a concerted effort to really keep the opportunities to a minimum."

"We were up 6–2 at the time, and we were all thinking, 'Let's kind of buckle down defensively,'" Kane said.

For all that buckling down, the Blackhawks couldn't keep Byfuglien from trying his best to beat Foster. With the teams skating four-on-four, the hulking defenseman forced a turnover, knocked the puck down, and took a wide-open wrist shot that hit Foster in his glove. More than four years later, Kane still remembered the save on Byfuglien.

"Wish I would've caught it," Foster said. "Would have looked really cool. But nonetheless, a save's a save. I can dress that up as the years go along."

It was one of two NHL-caliber saves Foster gives himself credit for. A minute after he turned aside Byfuglien's shot, he made his most impressive stop of the night when Laine made a backdoor pass to Paul Stastny, who was wide open on the doorstep. Foster slid over just in time to get in front of Stastny's one-timer—a shot that more than a few goalies even at that level wouldn't be able to stop on every occasion.

"He didn't get a lot of wood on it," Foster acknowledged. "But the pass goes across, I make a save across the ice, and I'm like, 'That's going to look cool.' That's a good save."

With less than two minutes left, Foster gobbled up a shot from Myers and held onto the puck while teammates on the bench tapped their sticks on the boards and fans cheered. Chants of "Foster! Foster!" reverberated off the walls of the cavernous building throughout the final 14 minutes of the third period.

"It was so much fun," Dineen said. "When you got a four-goal lead as the game wore down, you could see he made more saves, and the place was going bonkers."

Foster made his seventh save on Joel Armia with 1:25 remaining. Armia looked to the rafters and skated away.

"Somebody better be getting Foster a Foster's, that's for sure, with this performance," Olczyk said.

When the final horn sounded, Foster looked at defenseman Connor Murphy and shrugged. Murphy and the Blackhawks soon surrounded their fill-in goalie and celebrated a rare bright moment in a rough season.

"Just a crazy night," Kane said. "All anyone remembers about that is Foster coming in and stealing the show."

———————

After saluting the fans with the rest of Chicago's players, Foster tried to skate off but was told to put on a baseball cap and stay by the bench because he was the first star of the game. He wasn't a fan of the hat and didn't feel like he could put many words together in his postgame interview for TV and the arena loudspeakers.

"Scott, last night you were playing at Johnny's IceHouse, and tonight you make your NHL debut in front of this great crowd.

Describe what the last 24 hours have been like for you," rinkside reporter Michelle McMahon said.

"Well, it's a little different when a few hours ago you're working your day job and then you're living your dream," Foster said to more cheers. "It's fun."

Inside the Blackhawks' locker room, the fun was just beginning. Yelling and applause broke out in celebration when Foster entered, and there was no doubt who was getting the team's championship belt as the player of the game.

"I've got to give it to this guy," Forsberg said, handing Foster the belt. "A little different day for me, but I'll never forget it, so thank you," Foster said in his brief acceptance speech.

Before Foster took any of his gear off, he turned to VP of communications Adam Rogowin and asked for a picture. There would be plenty of professional photos from Foster's big night, but he wanted this one in his NHL jersey with a game puck on his cell phone.

"It was oddly important to me that I had that snapshot on my phone because it was mine," he said.

In the first and only postgame media scrum of his life, Foster had more one-liners for laughs than saves on the ice.

"The initial shock happened when I had to dress," he said. "And then I think you just kind of black out after that."

What are you going to tell your buddies at Golub tomorrow? "I made about 30 saves in a 1–0 win."

Did you see Joel Quenneville just laughing as you were getting on the ice? "I think I would, too."

Did Brent tell you you're only 999 behind him now? "Yeah, I think I'm just hitting my prime."

It sure was a long way from Western Michigan.

"Who would have thought?" Foster said. "You just keep grinding away in men's league, and eventually you'll get your shot."

Foster, even in the moment, didn't seem to lack for self-awareness.

"You think there'd be a lot of pressure," he said. "But really, tomorrow, I'm going to wake up. I'm going to button up my shirt and I'm going to go back to my day job. What pressure is there for me?"

Across the locker room, Seabrook joked that Foster stealing his spotlight summed up his career in a nutshell.

"It was pretty cool to see him go in there," Seabrook said. "The guys were saying when he was sitting in the locker room there he was cool as a cucumber, and he went up there and, Christ, took a few shots.

"I was like, 'Ooh, this guy looks pretty good.' But he was great. I think the boys were doing everything they could to try to help him out and he made some big saves. Fun night."

Quenneville at his postgame news conference quipped, "It was opening day for baseball, but we had to go to the bullpen a couple times today. It's interesting—something you don't see very often."

As interesting as it was for the Blackhawks and the rest of the hockey community, the Jets felt like they let a couple of important points slip away with the lackluster loss.

"It wasn't a good night," Little said. "It wasn't good from the start. It's one of those games you want to forget and put behind you and look to the next one."

After watching his team win its previous six games, scoring 23 goals in that span, Winnipeg coach Paul Maurice was none too pleased with the effort.

"There wouldn't really be a piece to the game that was at the level we've played at—or a level you need to play at—to have a chance to win in the NHL. I don't think it's any one thing," Maurice said. "The mental part of our game is to play at a certain rate, a certain pace, and we were well off that. We weren't very good."

Captain Blake Wheeler lamented that the Jets weren't prepared to play.

"We were just really slow," Wheeler said. "When you're slow, you shoot pucks into shin pads."

For all the self-flagellation, there was plenty of praise for Foster coming from the visiting locker room.

"It's probably something he dreams about, really special for him," Comrie said. "I really respect him for what happened. He went in and made some good saves."

Maurice said, "It's tough for anybody to come in 50 minutes into a hockey game, let alone a guy who hasn't played in the league. A great moment for him."

Once Foster finished another TV interview in the hallway, he walked back into the locker room that was now empty and remembered Parchman's message.

"Ghost town. Everyone's gone," Foster recalled. "So you had this split-second moment of Forsberg handing me the belt, me giving a thank-you to the guys for a crazy night, media, to now you're just standing in a room getting undressed by yourself."

Foster eventually found his way to the shower and on the way out told Rogowin he was done with the interviews. He didn't think he had any more to add to the story.

Foster made the 25-minute drive back to Oak Park and shared some smiles, laughs, and tears with his wife and parents. His parents wouldn't have been able to watch had they been back home in Sarnia because it was televised only regionally in Ontario and surrounding areas.

When he was unable to sleep, Foster turned on the TV and re-watched his game. He fast-forwarded through the first 45-plus minutes and hit play when he was entering the game. All the details he had no recollection of came back to him.

Foster finished watching his 14 minutes (and one second) of fame and was a man of his word. He got dressed, rode his bike to the station, and got on the train to go to work.

"Sitting at home was not going to be good for me," he said. "I got up and went in at the normal time. I didn't even go in late. And it's because I didn't know what else to do."

Foster worked that following Friday before the exhaustion caught up to him. On the way to celebrate a night out with friends and family the next night, he saw a FOSTER 90 jersey hanging in the front window of his local Gunzo's Sports Center. He walked inside and signed it for them and was on his way.

At a bar that night, a former neighbor joked that if Foster was shown on TV during the Blackhawks game at the Avalanche, she would make a scene. Sure enough, he was one of the stories of the night, and he spent time taking pictures with strangers.

That went better than Foster's next beer league game.

"I don't even know if I stopped my first shot," Foster said at the 2018 Blackhawks convention. "That didn't go great."

More than three years after reaching the NHL for a night, Foster still played in beer leagues two to three times a week, and in 2021 he resumed his role as one of Chicago's emergency backup goalies. He was reluctant at first to go back, realizing it would never feel the same.

"You realize that it is cool," he said. "It's neat to do and it's fun and it's a connection to hockey. For a period of my life, so much of it was a huge component of my life and I get a bunch of that with the guys that I play with, but it's not the same. You get a taste of that seriousness, and you want to get back to that game."

Scott and Erin's oldest daughter, Morgan, is a figure skater. Their youngest? Yeah, Wynnifred took up hockey not long after her dad's NHL appearance.

"[Morgan] started skating, tried hockey, watches the Olympics, sees figure skating, is attracted to it, goes into that," Scott said. "I don't care. Do whatever you want. Sports are awesome. Try them. Anything you want to do, try it."

Foster doesn't know if Wynni would have gone into hockey if not for his game with the Blackhawks. Morgan, at age five at the time, was already well up the figure skating path, but Wynni was two and started to figure out what her dad did for a night.

"Not only is Dad into hockey but we go to 'Hawks games and we've done 'Hawks stuff and I get to go to 'Hawks camps and it's a different thing for her," Foster said. "I always wonder if you're in the sport and doing this because you like it or are you doing it because you think I like it. I'm very conscious about making sure there's no pressure being placed on that element of it."

Wynni attended one of Kendall Coyne Schofield's girls hockey camps and could be on her way to following in her father's skate strides, even if he hopes she's not a goalie. But had Foster not played a game in goal for the Blackhawks, he wonders if his daughter would even be interested in the sport.

"It's neat seeing her do this stuff," he said. "I wonder back to— had that event not happened, would she be at Kendall Coyne's camp? Would we have taken her to Blackhawks camp? I don't know."

CHAPTER 7

THE ZAMBONI DRIVER: DAVID AYRES BEATS HIS HOMETOWN TEAM

DAVID AYRES' eyes lit up and he smiled.

"Am I going in?!" he asked.

Watching the Hurricanes play his hometown Maple Leafs on his phone in a locker room by himself in the bowels of the arena in Toronto, Ayres saw Carolina goaltender Petr Mrazek get run over and lie face down on the ice in distress. Hurricanes director of team services Pace Sagester saw the same thing and burst through the door, but even he wasn't yet sure what was happening.

The two had never met, and suddenly they were huddled over Ayres' phone watching to see what was happening a few hundred feet away on the ice. When they saw Mrazek doubled over in pain with head athletic trainer Doug Bennett guiding him to the tunnel, they looked at each other and knew it was time.

"*Hockey Night in Canada*, buddy," Sagester said. "No big deal. You're going in."

"For sure I'm going in?" Ayres replied. He put on a Carolina Hurricanes jersey for the first time and began the walk to the game that would change his life forever.

The youngest son of Bob and Mary Ayres just wanted to be like his dad and older brother, Chris. Bob Ayres was a goaltender, mostly playing in beer leagues with friends. Long before his goaltending career ended in his mid-forties because of a dislocated elbow, he had fostered the love of the position for his sons. And playing for so long also meant there was plenty of equipment around the house for Chris and David to put on a mask, pads, and play.

"We had some stuff hanging around which was too big for me, and then I ended up wearing it until it was too small for me," David said. "I was six when I was able to be a goalie full time. I thought, 'Let's do this.' That's all I wanted to do was just be a goalie."

Growing up in the 1980s in Whitby, Ontario, the kid known as David to his parents and Dave to his friends played recreational hockey up until high school when he had to choose. His ninth- and 12th-grade years, he played both and it was all encompassing, seven days a week. High school hockey was in the morning, with rec league games at night and no break. That took its toll.

"I totally burnt myself right out of hockey," Ayres said. "It just got really old."

He went to a couple of junior hockey camps and came away thinking he couldn't do it anymore. He didn't want to do it anymore. Bob Ayres went to watch David at one of the camps and said to his youngest son, "You're not even enthusiastic about hockey right now."

David at 18 years old was not enthusiastic at all. His brother had invited him to play with some of his friends, so he gave up the dream of making a career out of playing goaltender.

"I had more fun," Ayres said. "There's no stress. Just go out there and have fun playing hockey and hang out with your buddies, so it was way better for me. That's why I stopped playing competitively at that point."

With the prospect of David playing junior or professional hockey in his rearview mirror, Chris tried to talk him into joining him at the local General Motors plant, telling him he'd make good money. Seeing guys making $25 or $26 an hour was enough to convince David to take the job fresh out of high school. At 18 years old in 1995, he began a 36-month stretch of working overnight shifts putting truck parts together—instrument panels to bumpers and everything in between.

He had a routine, and naturally it involved hockey. David went to sleep at 8:30 or 9 AM, slept until the evening, went to the gym, and reported for work at 11 PM. He got Friday and Saturday nights off, played hockey on Sunday, and then went back to work Sunday night.

Ayres advanced to driving the forklift and supervising assembly lines. His time at GM lasted six years before the fatigue led him to try something different. A friend and his father were in the flooring business, so Ayres went to work with them. He began an apprenticeship in carpet and tile, working on industrial buildings all over the greater Toronto area. He was there for just over a year in the early 2000s when his life took a sharp turn.

Ayres thought he had a flu bug. He felt sick to his stomach while on the job two or three times a day and didn't know what was going on.

"I just couldn't shake it," he said. "I thought, 'I'm in really good shape, I'm 25 years old, there's nothing wrong with me.'"

It lasted for a couple of months, and Ayres started feeling worse and worse. Early in the winter of 2002, he was driving to work in the dark and through his dizziness did not spot a pedestrian who was trying to cross the road while he was turning.

"I didn't see them until the last second because I just kind of was out of it," Ayres recalled. "I slammed on the brakes and luckily didn't hit them or anything. I turned around and went home and I'm like, 'I need to go to the hospital. Something's going on with me.'"

He went to the doctor and the most basic of tests provided reason for alarm. Ayres' blood pressure, which is supposed to be around 120 over 80, was actually 240 over 120. The doctor told him to go to the emergency room right away to get checked out because Ayres was in danger of having a heart attack or a stroke at any time.

"Crazy me goes home," he said. "I was hungry. I needed something to eat, and then I went to the hospital later on."

After a battery of tests, doctors put Ayres on blood pressure medication that he took until May, when the sickness got worse. The high blood pressure made his legs and feet swell up so much that he had to open his Velcro flip flops almost all the way just to put them on.

"Just my toes would go kind of in there," he said. "My foot was like a balloon, and that's what I lived with."

When he went to a Federal Hockey League camp in Toronto in September 2003, it got so bad that Ayres couldn't even fit his feet into his skates because they were so swollen. He kept toughing it out until a breaking point on October 13, 2003.

He was at his parents' house for Canadian Thanksgiving. After dinner, he got up to leave and something didn't feel right. Leaning up against a wall, Ayres passed out. When he was conscious again, his parents told him to go to the hospital, and this time he didn't delay that trip.

At the hospital in Ajax, Ontario, Ayres underwent bloodwork and more tests, then waited four hours for the results to come back. When the doctor returned, the message was bleak.

"I've got some pretty bad news," he told Ayres. "You need a transplant. Your kidneys are failing. You need to go on dialysis right away, and you're going to need a transplant."

Ayres' mother, Mary, was by his side and immediately asked, "How do I get tested? How do I become a match?" The process would not be an easy one.

David wondered aloud, "OK, what do I do from here?" He was transported to a hospital 15 minutes away in Oshawa, Ontario, and put in a room by himself. A nurse joined him and sat there. Ayres had been given a book about kidney disease and transplants that explained the entire process, so he read it cover to cover to figure out what he was in for.

At one point, Ayres turned to the nurse and said, "You don't have to be here."

"I do have to be here," she said, explaining that some people who get the kind of news Ayres got fall into a dark state of mind and could attempt to kill themselves.

Ayres said that never crossed his mind. His only question was when he could get started.

"I wanted to get rolling," he said. "I thought it was going to be a quick process."

In the grand scheme of kidney transplants, it was quick. But the process of going through dialysis and living with the complications—"It sucked," Ayres said.

"The diet that you're on, it's horrendous. You have to stay off any kind of potassium, dairy—all that kind of stuff. They want you to eat so pure and they give you a whole program on what you can eat."

Ayres ate a lot of tuna from a can. Each time he returned home after dialysis, he wanted a tuna and cheese sandwich with a glass of milk. He wasn't supposed to drink any milk.

"It was the weirdest thing," he said. "It was just a craving I had."

He was limited to one liter of fluid a day. Over six-plus months of dialysis, he lost 40 pounds, going from 200 down to 160.

"You weren't filtering anything out and dialysis was taking all the liquid out of your body, so your heart just had to work super hard," Ayres said. "I was still thirsty."

All the while, he kept playing hockey.

Ayres had a water bottle on the back of his net while playing goal with a bunch of buddies in a winter league. But he wasn't allowed to drink it. He sprayed it in his mouth, swished the water around and spit it out. Despite wearing the heavy equipment, he didn't sweat during games because he was so dehydrated.

He enjoyed the sport so much more at age 26 than he did at the end of high school.

"It was hard to keep playing, but I wasn't about to give up hockey just because I was on dialysis and needed a kidney transplant," Ayres said. "I feel like you'd be a different player than you used to be, but you can still battle through it, so I kept playing."

Hockey also helped him through the long winter of dialysis. He had treatments on Tuesday, Thursday, and Saturday nights from 6 to 10 PM, and there was always a game on.

"So, I watched hockey," he said. "By the time they hook you up, put all the needles in and get you settled and stuff like that, the game's just about to start and then you watch the game and then you're ready to go home."

There was some fun hockey on, courtesy of his Toronto Maple Leafs. They trounced the rival Bruins 6–0 in Boston on Thursday, December 4, 2003, to extend their winning streak to seven games and wrapped up the regular season by beating the Ottawa Senators by the same score on Saturday, April 13, for their 45th victory.

The Maple Leafs played into May before losing in the second round to the Philadelphia Flyers. A year later and Ayres would have had no hockey to watch because the NHL lockout wiped out the entire 2004–05 season, and the Maple Leafs lost their next seven playoff series through 2022. Incredibly, he played a small part in one of those defeats, something he never would have figured while preparing for his kidney transplant.

Ayres got a kidney from his mother on May 20, 2004, at St. Michael's Hospital in Toronto. He was less than three months shy of his 27th birthday.

David said his mother tells him, "I gave you two lives." Based on his upbringing, he expected nothing less than the best from Mary and Bob Ayres.

"She always would do anything she could for her kids," David said. "My parents weren't rich parents. They're just kind of average, run-of-the-mill parents that would do absolutely anything for their kids. It was no surprise that my mom did that, but obviously it was huge when she stepped in and did that, for sure."

Nothing was easy for Ayres at that point, and his body rejected the kidney. He remained in the hospital for 21 days as doctors adjusted his medication to the point that everything in his body started working properly again.

Forget about playing hockey—the big incision in his stomach made it difficult for Ayres to walk. Trying to cross the street outside the hospital, he was in so much pain that it took him two traffic light rotations to make it.

"Cars were honking at me to get across the road and all this stuff, and I felt so bad," he said. "Even [on] the drive home, every bump that I hit it was just super painful."

───────────

Ayres was back in the gym doing light workouts by August. At times he went a little overboard and ripped open his scar. "It wasn't good for me," he said.

It took almost a year for him to get back onto the ice and two to feel like himself again in net. He was scheduled to attend a camp in Texas for the Central Hockey League's Laredo Bucks, but a buddy went in his place. Ayres never again tried to pursue playing hockey as a career.

Still, his path to the NHL emerged in a very different way from his first job after the transplant.

It was late 2004 and the University of Ontario Institute of Technology was opening a brand-new ice rink. A buddy's dad was the rink supervisor, and he asked Ayres if he had any interest in learning how to drive a Zamboni. Ayres worked a year at the rink at age 16, pushing nets, supervising public skates, and cleaning up dressing rooms.

"I always wanted to drive a Zamboni," he said.

Ayres spent about a year at the university rink before moving on to work for the city of Oshawa for six years. Ayres wanted to do something different. The American Hockey League's Toronto Marlies listed a building operator job for their arena, Ricoh Coliseum, and he applied for the job and got it in 2012.

The NHL was in the midst of another work stoppage in the fall of 2012, which meant more players skating with AHL teams. A couple of weeks into the new job, Marlies conditioning coach Mark Fitzgerald told Ayres to bring his goaltending gear to the rink because a handful of players needed someone to shoot on.

"I guess they thought I was OK of a goalie, so they asked me to come back the next day," Ayres said. "They needed a target."

Ayres continued showing up, and Marlies head coach Dallas Eakins told him to come out any time. He made more and more appearances and became the team's de facto practice goalie—even after leaving Ricoh Coliseum to become the manager of operations for Mattamy Athletic Centre at the old Maple Leaf Gardens in Toronto.

Organized hockey returned to Ayres' life in 2014 when one of his buddies talked him into playing in a senior league, Allan Cup Hockey. He was still skating and practicing with Marlies players and wasn't sure about getting back into competitive action. His buddy told him they needed a goalie because the team was terrible and warned him it was not going to be a great season.

Ayres agreed to play at age 37, but that warning turned out to be true. The Norwood Vipers had a lot of players who never reached the top tier of junior or pro hockey and did not fare well against more talented competition.

"We got trounced a lot of the times," he said. "It was a lot of fun. It's actually never fun losing. But it was a lot of fun hanging out with the guys. They were good guys. We stuck it out for the season. The season was a wreck for me."

Ayres lost all eight games he played and finished with an 8.88 goals-against average and .777 save percentage. But the "wreck" went far beyond the results. Ayres got pneumonia and shingles with a nasty finger injury thrown in for good measure.

While recovering from the bout of pneumonia, Ayres played an entire game in net, which he admitted later he should not have tried. Early in the third period of the Sunday game, an opposing player skated over the blue line and took a shot, and

Ayres was slow to react. He pulled his glove up before the puck got there, so that it hit him on the back of the glove and went in the net.

Ayres thought something felt weird, so he pulled the glove off to find the ring finger on his left hand dangling there. A tendon snapped off the back of it. He still has pictures to remember the moment by.

He went to see the Marlies team doctor the next day and was told he'd need to put the finger in a special splint and keep it there for eight weeks.

"Eight weeks?" Ayres asked. "I've got Marlies practice tomorrow. How am I going to do this for eight weeks?"

In true hockey fashion, Ayres taped up his finger, put it in his glove, and was back practicing with the Marlies on Tuesday, less than 48 hours after the injury.

"There was no quit," he said. "Just the passion and dedication I had for playing hockey was crazy."

Over his years with the Marlies, Ayres was pranked more than a few times by the equipment staff that he was needed for game action. Then came December 4, 2015.

He had called out sick from his job at Mattamy Athletic Centre that day because he wasn't feeling well. He was lying in bed when one of the Marlies equipment guys called him and told him to get all his stuff because he was needed for their game in Rochester, New York. Ayres laughed even as he was told this wasn't a joke.

"I don't believe you, man," he responded. "You've done this way too many times to me, and I'm not putting my stuff in my truck and I'm not driving to Rochester for no reason."

Another equipment manager called, and Ayres still wasn't sold. Then the phone rang, and it was Maple Leafs assistant general manager Kyle Dubas.

"Dave, no, we're serious," Dubas said. "We need you. So, get your stuff in the truck. Get driving."

Ayres left his home outside Toronto, got his gear, reached the U.S. border, and told the guard he was going to watch a hockey game. He diverted around an accident near the Buffalo airport and got to Blue Cross Arena in Rochester about 20 minutes before warm-ups started.

He got in a quick stretch, signed the one-day contract that allowed him to be in uniform, and stepped onto the ice for warm-ups.

"I look back at the pictures now and I see how pale my face was," Ayres said. "Normally I'm about 210 pounds. I was down to like 195 at that point and I got on the ice and you're nervous because I've played with these guys for years now but the first time you actually get into [uniform for] a game, the nerves start to kick in a little bit."

After years of being told "you're going to get into one," it was his first game in a Marlies uniform as he backed up Maple Leafs goaltender Jonathan Bernier, who was in the minors on an injury rehab assignment. Bernier stopped all 15 shots he faced through two periods and at the second intermission asked teammates, "Hey, do I let a bunch of goals in here in the third period so Dave can go in?" Ayres confidently told him not to ruin his shutout. Bernier stopped seven more shots in the third and the Marlies beat the Rochester Americans 4–0.

"I loved it," Ayres said years later. "Obviously it's something when you're growing up as a kid, you're like, 'I'd love to get into a professional game.' I thought it was going to be my one and only."

It took less than two months for Ayres to dress in a second AHL game for the Marlies. He was in the equipment managers' room at Ricoh Coliseum on the morning of February 27 when Dubas stopped by to say, "Dave, I might need you later tonight.

Don't leave." Sure enough, the Maple Leafs were trading goaltender James Reimer, and the domino effect opened a spot for Ayres to back up Antoine Bibeau for a home game against Rochester. The Marlies won 10–5.

"I was super pumped being able to dress at home," Ayres said. He also had his mask painted this time and "felt a little more legit."

Ayres kept working out at Ricoh Coliseum. He ran up and down the stairs and around the arena in a 40-pound vest. The equipment managers knew how hard he was working, and Ayres was part of the team.

"I was ready to go at all times," he said. "Then you get your two chances to back up, and I wish I would have been able to get into one of those two games. It would have been a lot more fun, but sitting on the bench was fantastic, too, right?"

Not getting into either of those games turned out to be fantastic for Ayres even though he did not know it at the time, because AHL experience would have blocked him from the opportunity of a lifetime.

———————

Ayres wasn't a one-sport wonder. He was involved in slow pitch baseball in his late thirties and played center field. During a tournament in London, Ontario, in July 2016, he met his now wife Sarah. They went to dinner on a Friday night after one of his games. In between their first date and second date Sunday, David tried out catcher for an inning and had a ball bounce up and hit his face, breaking his glasses and opening a cut under one of his eyes.

It was the last time he played baseball. He saw Sarah again on Sunday, and they were married 14 months later in September 2017.

"It's kind of funny how that whole thing worked," David said. "You saw off a baseball career and you start kind of a family at that point."

David and Sarah had been married more than two years by the time Saturday, February 22, 2020, rolled around. The NHL by this point had an emergency backup goaltender program that was more sophisticated than his happenstance opportunities with the Marlies, and David had reported for dozens of games at the Maple Leafs home arena over the course of three seasons. He even was one injury away once each for Toronto, Chicago, and Detroit but kept watching the game from a locker room.

Knowing the Maple Leafs' game against the Carolina Hurricanes was one of his games he was scheduled to be the emergency backup goalie for, David and Sarah enjoyed a relaxing morning before a regular workout at the gym.

"There was nothing really special that day," he said.

David figured it was a good day for a hefty leg workout and kept pushing himself with heavier and heavier weights. Sarah walked over midway through and said, "You're crazy. Why are you doing so much weight?" David brushed it off.

"I'm not going to play tonight," he said. "I'm not worried about it."

When they were driving to the arena, David had a premonition and said to Sarah, "Can you imagine if I have to go in? I have this weird feeling."

"Something was strange," he said years later.

David and Sarah got to the arena, parked in the garage, and took their usual place in the upper deck where they could stand and watch the game.

"We thought it was a typical night," Sarah said. "We had been through it so many times before."

In fact, Ayres dressed as the emergency backup goaltender for Carolina's AHL affiliate, the Charlotte Checkers, for a game at the Marlies exactly three weeks earlier.

———

The Hurricanes got into Toronto late Friday night after losing to the New York Rangers 5–2 back home in Raleigh and flying north. They were set to spend less than 24 hours in Canada's biggest city and the center of the hockey universe.

The Maple Leafs and Hurricanes were jostling for playoff position with roughly a quarter of the season left to be played and the trade deadline coming up Monday, February 24.

Toronto, now with Dubas in charge as GM of the NHL club, fired coach Mike Babcock 23 games into the season and players were still trying to find some consistency under Sheldon Keefe. The Maple Leafs played arguably their best game of the year their last time out, blanking the Pittsburgh Penguins 4–0 to end a brief losing streak.

Now four years removed from his trade from the Maple Leafs to the San Jose Sharks, Reimer was set to start for the Hurricanes against the team that drafted him. It was a big game for Reimer, and the spotlight of national television for *Hockey Night in Canada* on CBC only put more eyes on it.

"We sat around the hotel all day and went to the rink," said Sagester, who was responsible for coordinating the team's travel plans and media obligations. "All I was thinking about was the day off the next day, and I think everyone was, too."

Reimer's night got off to a bad start when Toronto forward Zach Hyman checked Hurricanes defenseman Jaccob Slavin into him 3:07 in. Reimer was down on the ice and Slavin called for medical attention. He tried to stay in the game despite the pain in his right knee.

"Every time I went down it hurt pretty good and it didn't feel right," Reimer said. "Unfortunately, that was the end of that."

Reimer pulled himself after making one more save.

"When Reims went out, you're not really worried because I've seen that 100 times," Hurricanes coach Rod Brind'Amour said.

David and Sarah Ayres watched it all unfold from their perch in section 317 at Scotiabank Arena. They saw Reimer call for a trainer and were glued to their phones making sure they weren't missing a call. The game was barely six minutes old when he got the call.

"Sure enough, they told him to go down," Sarah said.

They knew the deal. While David hustled down to the event level to assume the position as the next goalie up, Sarah contacted family and friends to let them know the situation so they could turn the game on if they weren't already watching.

Sagester left his spot in the press box, rode the elevator down, and went to the trainers' room so he could post an injury update on Reimer to the team's Twitter account. He kept peeking in while assistant athletic trainer Brian Maddox was working on Reimer. Maddox kept shaking him off like a catcher wanting a different pitch.

"It took a while to figure out if he was going to go back in or not," Sagester said.

Maddox finally emerged with the word: lower-body injury, will not return. Reimer said years later it was a sprained MCL.

Out on the ice, Mrazek, who faced 35 shots the previous night in the loss to the Rangers, was playing once again and it was his net because Reimer could not come back. The Czech Republic native stopped the first nine shots he faced, and the Hurricanes were peppering Maple Leafs goaltender Frederik Andersen at the other end of the rink.

Mrazek was perfect until a haphazard shift in the final minute of the first period. Mrazek made a left pad save on the initial shot from Toronto defenseman Jake Muzzin, then forward Alexander Kerfoot slid the rebound past him with 35.1 seconds left in the first to give the Maple Leafs a 1–0 lead. Carolina had 17 shots to Toronto's 10 at the first intermission.

Preparations were ongoing behind the scenes. While Ayres was in a locker room by himself getting some gear on just in case, equipment manager Bob Gorman got a white No. 90 CANES jersey ready. On a piece of paper in front of him was A-Y-E-R-S scratched out and the correct spelling A-Y-R-E-S written out instead.

Sagester saw Gorman piecing together the nameplate and realized he had forgotten all about his team's new emergency backup goaltender. He asked Gorman where the EBUG was and set off down the hallway. In the playoffs the year before, Carolina had a young goalie ready for a game at the New York Islanders just in case there were a couple of injuries, so he expected the same sort of thing this time around.

Busting through the door, he instead saw a 42-year-old who stood 6'0" tall and weighed 200 pounds. The men introduced themselves to each other quickly, and Sagester asked Ayres for some information: Can you spell your name? Where are you from? How old are you? Did you play professionally anywhere?

"I am not impressed with the answers he's giving me," Sagester recalled. "I'm like, 'Wait a second. This is very strange.' But I'm very impressed with him. He is so excited. Zero nerves."

Ayres told him he dressed for the Checkers earlier in the month, texted him a photo of his No. 34 Charlotte jersey, and added that he had a kidney transplant. Sagester tweeted from his account with photos: "The @Canes emergency backup goalie (EBUG) tonight is 42-year-old Dave Ayres. Ayres served as EBUG for the Charlotte Checkers on Feb. 1 against the Marlies, and received a kidney transplant in 2004."

Ayres asked if he'd get to keep his No. 90 Hurricanes jersey, which was special because the team stitched his name on the back. Each of the three previous times he was on call for an NHL team, the jersey—from the Blackhawks, Red Wings, and Maple Leafs—was left blank. Sagester said probably not. Ayres asked, "What about the nameplate?" and was told Gorman could talk about it after the game.

Sagester left the room and thought to himself, *This is the last time I'm ever going to see this guy.*

He was very wrong.

The second period was well underway at this point, with Mrazek in net for the Hurricanes and no one sitting on the bench in the backup goaltender spot. Ayres sat alone in an extra locker room watching the game on his phone.

The Hurricanes were putting on a clinic against the Maple Leafs. Lucas Wallmark finally cracked Andersen on their 25th shot of the game 5:46 into the second period to tie the score at 1. While Mrazek made easy work of the few shots he faced at the other end, Nino Niederreiter and Warren Foegele scored 56 seconds apart to give Carolina a 3–1 lead just past the midway point of the game. The Hurricanes were outshooting the Maple Leafs 31–16.

Then a seemingly innocuous play made all hell break loose. Toronto veteran Jason Spezza got his stick on a pass attempt from Joel Edmundson to fellow Hurricanes defenseman Haydn Fleury, and the puck deflected out of the Maple Leafs zone and toward Mrazek. Toronto's Kyle Clifford raced down the ice, Mrazek left the crease to play the puck far away in the left faceoff circle, and Clifford bowled him over, knocking Mrazek's mask off.

"What a collision here!" was the call from announcer Jim Hughson on Canada's national television broadcast. Hurricanes players went after Clifford, and a scrum ensued while Mrazek lay face down on the ice with Bennett scurrying over to attend to him.

Watching from up in the press box, Hurricanes general manager Don Waddell thought to himself, *Oh, heck, what do we do now?*

"You never think you're going to be in that spot," Waddell said. "You're looking for answers and you're looking for what do we do next. When Petr goes down, we have no options, so David gets his opportunity."

Hughson on *Hockey Night in Canada* called it "the worst-case scenario for the Carolina Hurricanes."

"The trainer's on the ice again to look at a goaltender and already one goaltender is out of the game," Hughson said. "We're just halfway through the second period, and David Ayres will be getting ready to play hockey. Might be needed tonight."

Sarah Ayres didn't even see the collision happen live. Her head was down still trying to reach friends and family to tell them to flip on the game. She heard the crowd react, texted her husband that the second goaltender was injured, and was overcome with nerves.

"I wish I could say I was excited, and I wasn't," she said. "I was so nervous. I was almost living vicariously through him thinking, 'OK, what's he going through? How is he dealing with this?'"

Hurricanes captain Jordan Staal was on the ice at the time, so he had a front-row seat.

"'Raz' got smoked, and it didn't look great," Staal recalled. "But you never really know how bad a body reacts to hits like that, and it was a pretty bad one. It didn't look like he was coming back any time soon."

Brind'Amour, a veteran of 1,643 NHL games as a player and more behind the bench as a coach, figured it out pretty quickly.

"You knew when Petr went down, he was out," Brind'Amour said. "Sometimes a goalie will be lying there and you're like, 'All right, he's going to get up.' That was obvious he was coming out."

Slavin thought to himself, *Aw, crap. What's going to happen here?* Staal looked toward the bench at Brind'Amour, who was pacing and looking around himself. For all his experience in hockey, he'd never been a part of anything like this.

"Your mind just went, 'Well, what's going to happen here?'" Brind'Amour said.

Fans buzzed with chatter around Sarah Ayres, asking each other what was coming next.

"I knew what was going on," she said. Probably more than anyone else in the crowd.

After watching Mrazek get run over, Sagester yelled, "Oh, shit!" and took off sprinting through the locker room and into the hallway. A security guard watching the game on a TV monitor asked, "Is he going in?"

"I don't know!" Sagester responded breathlessly, on his way to collect the person he never thought he'd ever see again.

Ayres was already standing up with half his goalie gear on. He saw what happened to Mrazek and was ready for this opportunity. He waited for it his entire life and came so close on many other occasions. All he had as any kind of confirmation was a text from Maple Leafs executive Reid Mitchell saying it was time to go in.

When Sagester busted through the locker room door once again, Ayres asked, "Am I going in?"

"Are you ready?" he said.

"Am I going in?" Ayres asked again.

"I don't know, man. Let's hold on a second," Sagester responded.

Ayres rushed to get dressed. As worried as his wife was at the time, he was calm.

"I wasn't nervous," Ayres said. "I wasn't afraid of anything. All those years—eight years of taking shots and taking shots every season basically, you just want to get a chance to get in there. And when you do get your chance, you want to try to capitalize on it as best you can."

There was no TV in the room, so Ayres and Sagester were glued to the tiny iPhone screen to find out what was happening. Then Mrazek was shown doubled over in pain skating off, flanked by teammates with Bennett's left hand on his back guiding him to the open door to the tunnel. Mrazek stepped off the ice and put his head down in pain. It was clear to everyone in the building he was done for the night.

Sagester looked at Ayres and deadpanned, "*Hockey Night in Canada*, buddy. No big deal. You're going in."

Ayres was greeted by Hurricanes goaltending coach Jason Muzzatti, himself a veteran of 62 NHL games in net. Muzzatti had rushed down from the press box to figure out what was going on. Ayres put his jersey on, and the visiting locker room attendant unlocked the door separating him from the rest of Carolina's team.

"You knew something special was happening," Sagester said. "No one knows what we're going to do. It's unprecedented."

The men started walking through the lounge when a voice yelling, "Ayres!" stopped them. It was Reimer, who was on the training table getting worked on. He hobbled over to talk to his new teammate.

"It's a great group of guys, man," Reimer told him. "You're going to do great. Don't worry about it."

Any semblance of nerves that had built up for Ayres was gone again.

———————

On the bench and the ice, the Hurricanes didn't know what to expect. NHL emergency backup goaltender rules that went into effect a few years earlier prevented equipment manager Jorge Alves from getting back in three years after his 7.6 second appearance because he worked for the team, and it couldn't be anyone with professional experience. But maybe some high-level experience?

"You're in Toronto. It was Saturday," Carolina forward Sebastian Aho said. "You think there's going to be maybe like a junior goalie who's right there."

His coach wondered the same thing.

"In my head I was thinking we were going to see a young kid come out, like an ex-junior player, and there was probably 20 in the stands watching the game," Brind'Amour said.

The Hurricanes' net remained empty for several minutes, but Ayres had time. Referees Marc Joanette and Tom Chmielewski were conferring with each other and linesmen Tony Sericolo and Scott Cherrey about Clifford's collision with Mrazek. They decided on a two-minute minor penalty for charging, and Maple Leafs fans booed the call while Clifford pleaded his case from the penalty box. Chants of "Ref, you suck!" emanated from the stands.

Keefe was not pleased with how his team was playing and had a message for them during the delay.

"If we don't change how we're playing, they don't even need a goalie," Keefe said. "There's no chances. There's no shots. There's nothing happening." He added later, "They didn't need a goal-tender the way the game was going."

While players were milling about on the ice, viewers watching from home had a better idea what was going on.

"What a night this could potentially become here with the two injuries to the Carolina netminders," rinkside reporter Kyle Bukauskas said. "David Ayres, an Ontario boy, played some Junior B hockey back in his day. He's 42 years old now, toiled around a couple minor league camps after that. He's been around the Maple Leafs and the Marlies for the last few years, a Zamboni driver and often during certain practices if they needed an extra body out there for a goalie, he'll fill in there. Their outdoor practice this year at Nathan Phillips Square, he was part of that, as well, so well familiar with the Maple Leafs organization and may be thrust into action tonight."

Following a security guard and with Muzzatti trailing him, Ayres emerged from the visiting locker room and began the trek down a few stairs and toward the ice.

Sagester said, "It feels like a gladiator walking in the Coliseum."

Then Ayres emerged from the tunnel with his Toronto Marlies mask and matching blue and white gear that would have made more sense if he were playing for the Maple Leafs. The crowd of 19,414 roared.

"I think when he came out and [was shown] on the screen and they saw the Marlies logo on the side of his helmet, it kind of gave them a little bit of an indication that he was with Toronto to begin with," Sarah said.

Much like Sagester, Brind'Amour wasn't impressed to see a 6'0" tall, 200-pound goalie as his last line of defense.

Welp, this is going to be interesting, he thought.

Niederreiter was the first to greet Ayres with a fist bump the moment he stepped on the ice. Other Hurricanes players skated over to give him a quick tap on the pads or pat on the chest to welcome Ayres to the NHL.

"Seeing him come out there I'm like, 'All right, well, we got a goalie and I guess we're moving on,'" Staal said. "That was basically it."

Brind'Amour shook his head with disbelief from his spot on the bench.

"Initially I'm thinking, 'We're playing a great game and we need the points,'" Brind'Amour recalled. "I wish we were down 5–1 and it wouldn't matter.... It's one of those nights where you're like, 'This is just going to end bad.' Let's just see what happens."

Ayres skated almost the length of the ice, reached the crease, and began stretching.

Hughson set the stage on TV: "Here he is in the National Hockey League in the middle of a playoff race for a team that desperately needs the points. What a moment."

Niederreiter and forward Martin Necas skated over to greet Ayres in net. A few pucks were thrown out, and Necas and Brock McGinn took some shots on Ayres to warm him up—something that was only allowed because he was an emergency backup who was not sitting on the bench.

"I just wanted to go in there and not make a mockery of myself when I went into the net," Ayres said.

By this point, Sarah was at ease watching from section 317.

"It was pure fear waiting for him to get on there," she said. "It was excitement once he stepped on the ice. I knew that this is what he worked for. He wanted this."

David had been on the ice for practice or a morning skate plenty of times. He always wondered what it would be like with the arena lit up for showtime and full of fans. While still down on his knees in the crease, he looked up to section 317 and the moment hit him.

"I was like: 'Cool, this is the view from down here. This is what it looks like from the ice full of fans,'" Ayres said. "I kind of just looked around a little bit and tried to take in as much as I could. And then, obviously, the game started."

––––––––––––

There was 8:41 left in the second period when the game resumed. Ayres figured to get a bit of time before he faced a barrage of Maple Leafs shots with the Hurricanes on a 5-on-4 power play and Clifford in the penalty box. When the puck was sent his way late in the power play, Ayres left his crease and calmly bounced it off the boards behind the net to Slavin like he'd been doing this in the NHL for years. Even if it wasn't good for their team, Maple Leafs fans cheered the textbook play by a guy most had never heard of.

He actually helped set up a goal. At the other end of the ice, Teuvo Teravainen shot the puck toward the net, and it bounced off Toronto defenseman Travis Dermott's left skate and inside the right post past Andersen. The goal with two seconds left on the power play gave Carolina a 4–1 lead.

Ayres squirted water through his mask and into his mouth from the bottle on the back of his net. More than 15 years removed from dialysis and his kidney transplant, he could actually drink it this time. But his moment of tranquility was soon shattered.

With Toronto's top line of Auston Matthews, William Nylander, and captain John Tavares on the ice and controlling the puck in the offensive zone, Hurricanes defenseman Brett Pesce injured his right shoulder trying to defend in the corner. Pesce went down in pain, leaving Tavares wide open to fire from the right faceoff circle and beat Ayres on the first shot he faced. The goal came just 19 seconds after Teravainen scored.

Oh, here we go, Slavin thought. He was the other defenseman on the ice for the goal.

Pesce blowing out his right shoulder was bad timing, but Ayres blamed himself for the goal by Tavares.

"It was my fault, so I just tried to shake it off," he said. "I knew that I overplayed that. Even though it was a good shot, I feel like I should have had it. I said, 'Just shake it off, Dave.' That's a tough one to come into the game and right away they score on you."

There was 6:43 left in the second period, and Carolina's lead was down to 4–2. A minute and a half later, it got worse for Ayres and the Hurricanes. The Maple Leafs skated the puck into the offensive zone, and Tyson Barrie's shot went off Carolina defenseman Jake Gardiner and right to Pierre Engvall in front. Ayres was down trying to stop the first shot, and Engvall had nothing but net to shoot into.

Oh man, what's going on right now? Ayres thought to himself. *That wasn't even my fault. I just missed it, and I knew I just missed it. That was a tough goal, but fair enough, man. Get in the game. It's your time to get in the game here. Don't make yourself look like an idiot.*

The Maple Leafs' goal song, "You Make My Dreams" by Hall and Oates, played over the arena speakers, and it was becoming a nightmare for Ayres.

Sarah was upset after the first shot went in. When the second goal was scored, she resigned herself to fate.

"I'm just going to sit here and I'm going to take this all in and enjoy it," she thought to herself. "It's obviously probably never going to happen again, and I sat there and said, 'Whatever's going to happen is going to happen.'"

Underneath the stands, Alves heard the goal horn go off twice in a matter of minutes and thought, *Oh no. This could have been the greatest night of his life. Instead he's going to give up a bunch of goals.*

Toronto had pulled to within 4–3 with 4:50 left in the second period after scoring on Ayres twice on its first two shots. Executives on other teams watching from afar started complaining about the Maple Leafs potentially being gifted a victory in the middle of a heated playoff race because they were facing someone who was not an NHL goalie.

Florida Panthers general manager Dale Tallon knew from his own chaotic experience in 2015 and the meetings and conversations that followed exactly what the rule was.

"What else are you going to do? That's just the way it is," Tallon said. "Where else are you going to get a guy to stop the puck?"

At the time, the Hurricanes didn't have much faith in Ayres stopping the puck. They thought they were about to get blown out.

"The first two shots go in, it's never a good feeling," Staal said. "We weren't expecting much out of it. Obviously, it's hard to come in cold in an NHL game. We're all human, and we were all thinking it."

Aho called it "kind of like a hopeless situation."

Forward Erik Haula skated over to Ayres and told him, "Just have fun. We don't care if you let 10 goals in." Slavin at the time also realized this game was different.

Behind the scenes, there was panic. Muzzatti called Hurricanes forward Ryan Dzingel, who was sitting up in the press box as a healthy scratch, to see if he'd be willing to put on goalie pads and go in net. Unbeknownst to the coaching and training staffs, Reimer started putting his gear back on and was convinced he could tough it out and at least stand up in net and block the puck.

"I would have been pretty much a standup goalie. I could go down on the other knee maybe," Reimer said. "As a competitor,

Carter Hutton gives the Philadelphia Flyers jersey off his back to season ticket holder John Demchuk after a game late in the 2009–10 season, his first game in an NHL uniform. (Photo courtesy John Demchuk)

The Flyers' Brian Boucher celebrates with teammate Kimmo Timonen after the team beat the New Jersey Devils on March 28, 2010—the game in which Hutton dressed. (AP Photo/Matt Slocum)

Hutton's Flyers jersey from his first NHL game in uniform hangs in a frame in his parents' house in Thunder Bay, Ontario. (Photo courtesy Jack Hutton)

Now suiting up for the Nashville Predators, Hutton gloves a shot by the Flyers' Wayne Simmonds during a shootout on January 16, 2014, in Philadelphia. (AP Photo/Tom Mihalek)

Carolina Hurricanes equipment manager Jorge Alves warms up after signing a contract to dress as an emergency backup for the team's game against the Tampa Bay Lightning on New Year's Eve 2016 in Tampa, Florida. (AP Photo/ Mike Carlson)

Alves (40) is congratulated by Joakim Nordstrom (42), Lee Stempniak (21), and Noah Hanifin (5) following his NHL debut against the Lightning. Tampa Bay won 3–1. (AP Photo/Mike Carlson)

Young Scott Foster plays for the Port Edward Blackhawks. (Photo courtesy Scott Foster)

oster holds up a game puck after appearing or the Chicago Blackhawks as an emergency ackup goaltender against the Winnipeg Jets n March 29, 2018. (Photo courtesy Scott oster)

Foster poses in front of his locker stall after stopping all seven shots he faced as an emergency backup goaltender for the Chicago Blackhawks. (Photo courtesy Scott Foster)

Carolina Hurricanes emergency backup goaltender David Ayres puts on his jersey before going into the game against the Toront Maple Leafs. (Photo courtesy Pace Sagester)

Ayres prepares to leave the locker room to enter an NHL game for the Carolina Hurricanes. (Photo courtesy Pace Sagester)

Ayres speaks with Sportsnet's Kyle Bukauskas on *Hockey Night in Canada* after beating the Maple Leafs as the Hurricanes' emergency backup goaltender. (Photo courtesy Pace Sagester)

Hurricanes coach Rod Brind'Amour congratulates Ayres after the team's victory in Toronto on February 22, 2020. (Photo courtesy Pace Sagester)

Ayres holds up his No. 90 Carolina Hurricanes jersey while on set at *The Late Show with Stephen Colbert*. (Photo courtesy Pace Sagester)

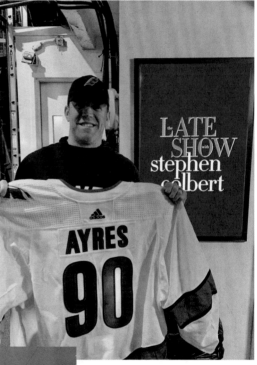

Ayres meets with NHL commissioner Gary Bettman at his office in New York on February 24, 2020. (Photo courtesy Pace Sagester)

Dallas Stars left wing Jamie Benn (14) greets Anaheim Ducks EBUG Tom Hodges (86) at the end of the game in Dallas on the final day of the 2021–22 NHL regular season. (AP Photo/ LM Otero)

Arizona Coyotes backup goalie Nathan Schoenfeld, left, signed to the team only hours prior to the game due to an injury to goalie Anders Lindback, sits next to Shane Doan during the second period of a game against the Montreal Canadiens on February 15, 2016. (AP Photo/ Ross D. Franklin)

Washington Capitals backup goaltender Brett Leonhardt warms up before a game against the Ottawa Senators on December 12, 2008, in Washington. Leonhardt, a 6'7" website producer for the Capitals, dressed as the team's backup goalie for the game against the Senators because of an injury to Jose Theodore. (AP Photo/Luis M. Alvarez)

Coyotes backup goalie Tom Fenton, right, watches teammate Scottie Upshall (8) play against the New York Rangers during the first period the game on December 16, 2010, in New York. He was in a barber's chair when he got the call. (AP Photo/Frank Franklin II)

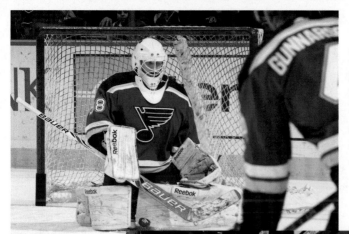

Emergency backup goaltender Tyler Stewart takes warm-ups for the St. Louis Blues prior to their game on December 7, 2017. (Photo courtesy Tyler Stewart)

Stewart stands on the bench prior to the team's game on December 7, 2017. (Photo courtesy Tyler Stewart)

A plaque featuring photos of Ben Hause in a New Jersey Devils jersey on Santa's lap as a child and Hause in his Devils jersey as an emergency backup goaltender hangs in his home. (Photo courtesy Ben Hause)

you always want to try and be there for your team. I tried to see if I could make a go of it."

He started stretching and knew he shouldn't go back in, and Maddox told him as much, but the Hurricanes were working on a Plan C just in case the game snowballed.

"It wasn't in the cards," Reimer said. "It didn't look like it was going to be a good situation."

Brind'Amour was thinking like a coach. He just wanted to get through the almost five minutes before intermission so the entire team could reset. That's all Ayres wanted, too, and he told his teammates that. The Hurricanes obliged, not allowing a single shot on net on a Maple Leafs power play when Haula was penalized for slashing and then shifting the focus when Edmundson fought Clifford as payback for running over Mrazek. Seconds after the fight, Ayres stopped a shot from Matthews from 11 feet out. Foegele dived into the crease to make sure the puck wouldn't slide in, and Ayres froze it to stop the clock. It was his first save in the NHL and kept the score from being tied with a minute left in the second. He didn't face another shot the rest of the period.

"I was thankful that they got me to the intermission without too many more tough scoring chances," Ayres said. "They did a good job in front of me."

The second period horn sounded with the Hurricanes still up 4–3. Brind'Amour felt like his team had a slim chance to win and went into the coaches' room with a clear message.

"I know we lose if we say we got to protect the goalie," he said. "I know we lose. Zero chance we'll win. So, we have to go the other way and be like, 'Let's try to get five goals this period' and come with that mentality and see what happens."

At the same time, inside the locker room the mood was much different. Aho described it as hilarious.

"Guys were laughing," he said. "It was very unusual. Usually guys are pretty focused and doing their own thing, but this time everyone was making jokes and trying to get him feeling more confident and comfortable in there. It was definitely one of those moments that you will remember forever."

Reimer reprised his role as Ayres' hype man. Still hobbling through his injury, Reimer worked his way over to Ayres' stall and said, "Hey, you're a goalie. You know what you're doing out there. They wouldn't put you in this position if they didn't think you knew what you were doing. Don't worry about everything else that's going on around you, all the fan noise and stuff. Try and block that out and just make saves and enjoy the game."

Ayres had gotten the reset he wanted and was in a calmer state of mind. He also got a wardrobe change. Alves forgot that Ayres was wearing Toronto blue and asked him to put red shells over his goalie pants to match the rest of the uniform. There wasn't much they could do about the blue and white mask, glove, blocker, and pads.

Then Brind'Amour walked in and rallied the troops, telling the Hurricanes to play for their new goaltender and do it for Ayres.

"He came in there and he just said, 'This is going to be a once-in-a-lifetime kind of thing for most of you guys, especially for Dave. Let's go out there and win this one for Dave,'" Ayres recalled. "The guys just jumped right on board. And it was really cool of him to say that and to acknowledge me, that I was actually in the game and we had a chance to win this."

Brind'Amour also had a strategy to go with his inspirational message: *Don't allow any quality scoring chances and go on the offensive.*

"Roddy always seems to be able to push the right buttons for guys," Staal said. "As a group, we knew if we had a great third period that we would be part of something special and something really cool not only for Dave but around the league and around hockey. The boys were confident that we could pull it off."

Less than a minute into the third period, the Hurricanes got some breathing room. Foegele forced a turnover by Tavares, got the puck, and powered to the net to score his second goal of the game. Just 53 seconds out of intermission, Carolina led 5–3.

Early in the period, Ayres actually got credit for a shot for clearing the puck all the way down the ice toward Andersen. Then he had to focus on a shift three minutes in. Matthews skated through defenders and put the puck on net from a bad angle, and Ayres stuck it away. Mitch Marner chopped a backhanded attempt toward the net, which Ayres made a pad stop on before scooping up the puck with his glove. Maple Leafs fans in attendance cheered each save by the opposing goaltender.

Also cheering for Ayres? Scott Foster, who grew up rooting for the Maple Leafs and still followed the team as an adult. It had been less than two years since the Chicago-area accountant's NHL debut as the Blackhawks' emergency backup goaltender against the Winnipeg Jets in which he stopped all seven shots he faced to make some hockey history.

Foster was out with his daughters and had been following the Hurricanes–Maple Leafs game on his phone. He knew about the injuries to Reimer and Mrazek and his phone soon filled up with messages. Watching Ayres step in like he did in 2018 made a flood of emotions come back, and Foster could not sit down the rest of the game.

"I stood behind my sofa in my living room with this game on, and I was more nervous watching that game than playing in my game," Foster said. "If I'm watching that entire game, I'm cheering for the Leafs. I instantly was cheering for David Ayres.

Everything that was happening, it was pins and needles. It was intense."

At one point, Foster thought, *There's one other person that knows what he's going through right now, and it's me.*

Much like Foster did for Chicago, Ayres began to settle in. He just wanted some action.

"It was just about being able to make a couple saves," he said. "When the Leafs had the puck at center ice, the fans were just yelling, 'Shoot! Shoot!' And I'm thinking in my head, 'Yeah, shoot. I'm ready for shots.' That's what I was hoping for: more shots make you feel more comfortable obviously if you're able to make saves."

Ayres was up to three saves on five shots. Years of practicing with the Maple Leafs and Marlies prepared him for this opportunity.

"This is good," he thought. "I know where these guys are going to shoot. I've got some of the tendencies, so that's helpful.

"If I played against a team that I didn't know anybody on, I would be just kind of guessing the whole time and hoping I'm making the right move, making the right save."

Before Ayres had the opportunity to face another shot, the Hurricanes gave him some more insurance. Haula dived to try to chip the puck in; it banked off the crossbar. Necas outraced Tavares to the loose puck and backhanded it into the empty side of the net too fast for Andersen. Only 3:44 into the third period, Carolina now had a 6–3 lead.

Ayres made another save on Matthews not long after Necas scored, and minutes later he faced a shot that elite NHL goalies don't stop much of the time. Kerfoot found Hyman for a one-timer from the slot 29 feet from the net.

"They've done that before in practice," Ayres said. "I've seen them do that a few times. I saw it being set up where he cut through the middle, and I just made sure I got there. I was just kind of hoping it was going to hit me in the chest."

It was actually even more difficult than that. Ayres had to slide over and caught the puck between his body and the blocker on his right hand, squeezing it so it couldn't get through.

Reimer, Muzzatti, and others watched from the lounge adjacent to the locker room and slowly began to realize what was unfolding out on the ice.

"The minutes are slowly ticking by, and it feels like an eternity," Sagester said. "None of us are really even letting us believe that it's going to happen because it could turn in a second, obviously. He could allow three goals on three shots any minute, and that would have been that.

"We knew we were experiencing something that we would remember for the rest of our lives as it was happening."

They high-fived after each save and shared a common thought: *Can you believe this is happening?*

The saves kept coming. Ayres stopped Kerfoot on a tip attempt with 10:56 left. He turned away Spezza's wrist shot with 3:47 left. But he didn't face a barrage of shots from the Maple Leafs because they had no room to even get into the attacking zone.

"Toronto came across the [blue] line and they had to dump it in, and the guys were on it right away," Ayres said. "One of the [Maple Leafs] guys had no option and he just put it off the glass and out and the forward just forechecked like crazy down the ice. I was just like, 'These guys are in it. They're ready to go. They're not letting anything get to me.'

"Whether or not they didn't want goals scored on them, they didn't trust me because I was letting goals in or whatever the reason was, they played so well in front of me."

Something about the circumstances of the night and the season knocked the Maple Leafs off their game, and Brind'Amour knew that. But part of that was how the Hurricanes were defending and turning up the pressure.

"It was just taking that desperation to the highest level," Brind'Amour said. "Coaches always talk about it all the time, but when it's real it's so obvious. We had to play like that. There's no bailing you out."

Slavin called it easily the best period of hockey the Hurricanes played that season.

"Part of it, Toronto's got to be in a weird headspace going into that third period, as well," he acknowledged. "I think it's probably a little bit of both—we played really well, but for them they're like, 'Oh man, this is so weird.' We locked down. We did everything that we could to not let that puck get in our zone."

It might have been one of the best periods of hockey ever played in the NHL. Brind'Amour said, "I could've been in there and we would've won the game."

Carolina allowed Toronto just seven shots in the final 20 minutes.

"The way we played in that third period was how we always want to play, and it's just not giving up anything," Staal said. "That's always a goal. And you're going to create offensive plays playing like that.

"It was definitely the way we wanted to play, and obviously Dave made some big saves for us, as well, to kind of finish it off."

When the final few minutes were ticking away in the third period and the adrenaline began to wear off, Ayres began to feel the effects of his heavy leg day at the gym. He powered through.

Fittingly, the final save came on Clifford, the player whose collision with Mrazek made it all happen. Ayres caught the harmless shot from 43 feet out, just inside the blue line. The save on Hyman was his favorite, but he knew he'd always remember his final stop.

"In my head I was thinking, 'I'm not letting go of this puck,'" he said. "This is probably my only chance to ever get in the NHL and this is going to be my game puck, so I'm going to keep it."

Ayres held the puck in his glove as the clock hit 0.0. Hurricanes teammates flooded over from the bench, mobbing him and bouncing up and down in celebration like they just won a playoff series.

"Those are the games, those are the moments in your career that you'll remember forever," Slavin said. "Those won't be ones that you forget, and those are the ones that are special."

Ayres was named the first star of the game and saluted the crowd that he turned into Hurricanes fans for a couple of hours.

———

Keefe made short work of his exit from the bench and walked up the tunnel after the most improbable of losses. He was plenty familiar with Ayres as a practice goalie from his tenure with the Marlies and the start of his stint with the Maple Leafs but never expected to get beaten by him in an NHL game.

"He comes to the rink every day and just wants to work and wants to be a part of it, and whether it's with the Marlies or the Leafs he's always there when you need him," Keefe said that night. "There's probably not an emergency goaltender anywhere in pro hockey that's seen this many pro shots as this guy. He's in pretty much every day getting work. It feels pretty terrible given that he's on the other side today from our end of it, but on a personal note, you can't help but feel pretty darn good for the guy."

The mood in the home locker room was somber. Toronto had wasted what looked like an easy opportunity to pick up a win and add two valuable points in the standings to solidify the team's playoff chances.

"We obviously didn't handle the circumstances of the game very well," Tavares said. "It might've been our poorest night of execution. We seemed like the team that played last night and traveled. We were sloppy."

Matthews lamented that "the effort wasn't there." Marner described his own effort as "dog shit." He toe-picked for the first time in decades and questioned if the willpower was there for the Maple Leafs.

"We were not good enough," Marner said. "Everything just seemed to go wrong."

In true hockey fashion, players were quick to credit the Hurricanes, who got in shot lanes, sacrificed their bodies to get in the way of pucks, and outworked the Maple Leafs for much of the game.

"Regardless of who was in net tonight, they did a really good job of keeping us on the perimeter for the most part," Matthews said. "No disrespect to Davey. Awesome goalie. But when you have an emergency goalie like that come in a game, I think the consensus is to shoot the puck as much as possible. I think that was the case there in the second, and they just locked down."

Ayres actually agrees with that. Even now, it bothers him when people say he beat the Maple Leafs.

"If you watch the game, I didn't beat them at all," Ayres said. "It was the rest of the Carolina team that beat them. They kept the shots to a minimum and the chances to not easy chances, but I didn't have any two- or three-shot rebounds sort of thing. They did their job."

That job made life difficult for Toronto. Keefe in his post-game news conference said the game didn't change when Ayres replaced Mrazek.

"It just so happened it was a different guy in the pipes," he said. "The game was the same. They just continued to play hard the way that they were before, and we couldn't get to him."

Toronto had lost three of its past four and seven of its past 11 games with the trade deadline up next.

"It's a tough one," Keefe said. "It'll be a tough one here for us to regroup from. It's going to take a little time."

The feeling down the hallway was the polar opposite. Ayres became the first emergency backup goaltender to record a victory in the NHL and the oldest NHL goalie to win his debut. The famous *Hockey Night in Canada* towel was draped around his neck for the national television interview with Bukauskas. Ayres said it was "the time of my life out there."

Ayres had more postgame media obligations, but they could wait. His Hurricanes teammates couldn't. Brind'Amour gave him a big hug and said, "Go in there, buddy. They're waiting for you."

Ayres walked into the room with all his gear on and his mask pulled up over his face. The second he entered, players doused him with water from every bottle they could find. A couple even hopped up on locker stalls so they could spray water on Ayres like he just won the Hurricanes the Stanley Cup

"That was our goalie," Staal said. "The boys were kind of champing at the bit just to get a piece of him and congratulate him on a great win."

With Ayres smiling from ear to ear after the most unforgettable 28:41 of hockey in his life, players jumped up and down, applauded, and shouted, "Davey!" Reimer shuffled over and gave Ayres a hug. It was the last thing he expected.

"I had no idea I was going to get a shower before I got in the shower, but I got one," he said minutes after.

Ayres thought by the time he got back into the room that players would be out of their gear and packing up to go home. Not a chance.

"Guys were just wanting to celebrate with him the best that we could," Slavin said. "We didn't have champagne in the locker room for him, so guys just got the waters going."

Brind'Amour watched the scene unfold from the edge of the room, brushed water off his suit, and walked in for a once-in-a-career postgame speech.

"I'll tell you what, I'll be quick here," Brind'Amour said. "There's not often in a game that you get tied to a great memory. Fuck, that's why you do this. You'll see when you're done. You'll look back. All you'll have is the memories that you got. And you just gave me one. You gave each other one. But that's a fucking memory that I'm going to have forever.

"The way you guys played that fucking third period, for you," he said, pointing to Ayres, "and the way you played for us." Applause and more shouts of "Davey!" interrupted briefly.

"I'm proud of you guys," Brind'Amour continued. "I don't know what your song is but, fuck it, play a song. Great job." He gave Ayres a thumbs up and left the rest of the celebration to the players.

Ayres put on a dry shirt and talked to dozens of reporters fascinated by one of the best stories in sports. Once it was all done, he said, "It's going to be good to go home and kind of relax."

———

Relaxing would have to wait. Hurricanes general manager Don Waddell called Sagester to ask if Ayres could come to Raleigh for their next home game the following Tuesday night as a show of appreciation. A New York City media circuit was being planned for Monday for the Zamboni driver who got into an NHL game and won.

In the immediate aftermath of the victory Saturday night, Ayres was the toast of Toronto. He took pictures with Hurricanes equipment managers and others and received a 24-pack of Molson Canadian beer from the locker room attendants. Carolina's coaching staff gave him a bottle of wine that Brind'Amour autographed.

In addition to staying young by practicing with professionals, Ayres said one of his secrets was that he drinks alcohol sparingly and never beer.

"I don't smoke, I don't drink, I work out almost every day, and I just like that lifestyle," he said. "Don't get me wrong; I don't eat perfect, but I don't eat bad either."

David finally saw Sarah hours after the game was over and the circus atmosphere had died down. She told arena employees who she was, and they let her meet up with her husband just outside the Maple Leafs locker room.

"He did really well," Sarah said. "I was proud of him. He played a lot differently than what he normally does. I guess he was anxious. He said he felt the ice move out from underneath him when the fans were yelling and screaming. It's a very different situation than just being in practice."

With some help, David and Sarah loaded the beer, jersey, his equipment, and other gifts into the truck. Over the following weeks, David gave the beer away to friends who came over but still to this day has not opened the bottle of wine.

He still takes kidney medication twice a day and goes for regular blood work check-ups.

"Most of the days you don't even realize that you had a kidney transplant," Ayres said. "You just wake up in the morning and you take your pills, you put your deodorant on, and that's your routine.

"You have good days, and you have bad days, but you're happy you're alive. You're happy you're able to get out there and do everything that you used to be able to do beforehand."

That includes hockey, even if it's no longer as a practice goaltender for the Maple Leafs or Marlies. He didn't have any interest in resuming his role as an EBUG, either, when the program returned for the 2021–22 season. Before making a cameo appearance at Marner's charity event in the fall of 2021, Ayres rented out some ice so he could practice taking some shots. Still, "I was just atrocious in the charity game," he said. "I think I forgot how to play goal altogether."

Ayres remembered not long after. By late 2021, he was still playing recreational hockey every Wednesday and Friday night with friends, who feel like his goaltending is back to peak form. He credits that to not beating himself up by going on the ice just about every day like the 2019–20 season.

When he was doing that, his knees took a beating. During one Marlies practice, he felt something pop in his right knee and didn't want to say anything because he wanted to stay on the ice.

"For me it was just like, 'You're a goalie, you're going to get hurt all the time, your knees are going to get bad, your hips are going to get bad,'" Ayres said. "All that kind of stuff was always just sore and then it would go away, and then it was sore, and it would go away. It was just something I dealt with."

His knees were so banged up that occasionally that season, he needed Sarah to pull his arms forward to help him get off the couch. He didn't let on how bad his knees were and even felt some tweaks during his one and only NHL game.

But Ayres wasn't going to let that pain keep him from playing.

"You couldn't not be there when the guys wanted you on the ice," he said. "I kept playing."

Much like Foster never figured he'd be the last EBUG to get into a game, Ayres does not want that distinction forever.

"I kind of hope that someone else after me gets another chance and does the same thing: goes out there and shows everybody that there's a guy that can jump in," Ayres said. More than two years later, he was pulling for Tom Hodges when the life insurance salesman entered the Anaheim Ducks' season finale at the Dallas Stars.

Ayres also had a significant impact on the playoff race, after all. Had the Maple Leafs beaten the Hurricanes in regulation, they would have faced the New York Rangers instead of the Columbus Blue Jackets in the qualifying round of the expanded, 24-team playoffs the NHL put together after the season was suspended because of the pandemic.

Carolina beat New York to advance. Toronto lost to Columbus, continuing the drought of playoff-round losses that dated to 2004.

CHAPTER 8

THE INSURANCE SALESMAN: TOM HODGES MAKES MORE HISTORY

IT WAS NOT THE FIRST TIME Tom Hodges was in nearly this exact spot.

Among his 100-plus games serving as an emergency backup goaltender in Dallas, he had been called down to one of the locker rooms to get ready four previous times. Twice when the Stars needed him to get ready and once when the Anaheim Ducks weren't sure if John Gibson would be able to stay in a game.

The first time, Gibson decided he was good to go, and Hodges returned to his place in the stands. On April 29, 2022, it was a far different outcome.

It was the final day of the 2021–22 NHL regular season, and the Stars were playing one final game before starting the playoffs. They could still move up in the standings with a victory and a loss by Nashville at lowly Arizona.

The Ducks took a 1–0 lead on a goal by Max Comtois 7:33 into the first period. The Stars failed to tie it when Jason Robertson clanked a shot off the post and went into intermission trailing.

Anthony Stolarz led Anaheim onto the ice for the second period because Gibson was injured and couldn't continue. Hodges got the call while he was eating in the stands and left his seat to begin the preparations to enter an NHL game.

Even then, the 27-year-old life insurance salesman originally from the United Kingdom didn't expect much more to come of it.

Originally from Shropshire outside Birmingham in the United Kingdom, Hodges traced his love of hockey to a visit to a mall as a child.

His father was being transferred to the U.S., and Hodges did not want to leave his home country. A visit to Stonebriar Centre mall in Frisco, Texas, changed the course of his life.

Hodges saw other kids playing hockey and knew it was for him.

"I just fell in love with the sport," he said. "It was the first sport that I had ever really had any interest in at all. I just knew for some reason that I had to play."

After the move was complete, Hodges at age 11 spent several months learning how to skate and all about the fundamentals of the game. He and his family were only supposed to be in Texas for a couple of years, but they stayed, and he decided to become a goaltender.

He dreamed about one day playing in the NHL but a freak accident—a puck to the head at age 12—caused Hodges to lose the sight in his left eye. Hodges did not go totally blind in the eye, but enough of his vision was gone to dash those hopes.

"It became an impossibility," he said. Or so he thought.

Hodges played some under-18 minor hockey and for Plano West High School. Wanting to stay close to home to be near his mother, who was battling cancer, Hodges enrolled at Southern Methodist University and majored in journalism with a minor in sports management.

After a few years away from the game, he wanted to get back into it—perhaps just to join an adult league and have some fun. His path to the NHL resumed when he got back on the ice and started working with Tom Speer, who happened to be the goalie coach for the Allen Americans, a nearby minor league team in the ECHL.

Hodges impressed enough that Speer invited him to skate with the team. The Americans were in need of an extra goalie, so Hodges signed an amateur tryout contract in January 2017 so he could go on the road and be around the team. Not long after, he appeared in one ECHL game for Allen and did not allow a goal in his handful of minutes on the ice and sealed a victory.

"I think I led the league in goals against that year," Hodges said.

A few EBUG scares followed during his time in the ECHL, and the NHL put in its rule to make sure there was a goalie in each building capable of entering a game if needed. Speer sent Hodges' information to the Stars, and assistant general manager Mark Janko called to invite Hodges to serve in that role.

"With that position you need somebody who works extremely hard at practice and also realizes that he's out there for the team and not himself," Janko told SMU's *Daily Campus* in 2019. "He understands that and embraces that mentality."

Hodges split his time practicing with the Americans and the Stars, thinking little of the possibility of facing his adopted hometown team in an NHL game someday.

———————

Hodges was getting dressed in an area of the visiting locker room at American Airlines Center when one of Anaheim's equipment managers approached and told him, "Hey, I think you need to get dressed a little faster."

"A wave of fear just washed over me, which I think is pretty normal," Hodges said.

Stolarz was struggling with his own injury during the second period when he allowed goals to Dallas defensemen Thomas Harley and Joe Hanley. Troy Terry tied it for the Ducks, who were dealing with the uncertainty surrounding Stolarz and the possibility of turning to the local EBUG in Game 82 of the regular season.

No one was quite sure if Hodges would be needed. The time dragged in the bowels of the arena while the game was going on.

"There was probably 30 minutes there where it was like 50/50 whether or not I was going to have to go in," he said. "By far the hardest part was not knowing."

Unbeknownst to the crowd in Dallas and those watching on TV, it was clear by the second intermission that Hodges would need to enter the game. He found out Stolarz could barely walk and was told to put on his jersey.

It was the most nervous he had ever been in his life.

Hodges slipped on a blank white No. 68 Ducks jersey. There wasn't even enough time to attach his name to the back of it.

Through all the nerves, his new teammates for a night provided some solace.

"They just came up to me, trying to calm me down," Hodges said. "They said they don't care—win, lose, let in 10—'Just go out there and have fun.' I think that made the whole experience a lot easier."

Instead of the goalies Anaheim leaned on all season, a 5'10" life insurance salesman led them out for the third period of a game that was tied and still meant something to Dallas. Wearing a Stars mask and gear in his opponent's colors, Hodges slid onto his knees in the crease and did his usual routine to get ready.

Ten seconds before puck drop, Hodges asked Terry what the score was. "It's 2–2, but don't think about it," he responded.

"Our attitude shifted to playing for him," Terry said afterward. "You could tell he was nervous. We just tried to calm him down.... We were going to be happy no matter what happened."

A sense of calm fell upon Hodges when the puck dropped.

"Hockey is something that I've been doing my whole life, so that was a little bit more normal," he said. "Once I touched the ice and everything, it was a little bit easier."

It took more than six minutes for the Stars to get their first shot on goal. Roope Hintz let a wrist shot go from the right faceoff circle, and Hodges slid over and calmly made a left pad save to send the puck into the corner.

"He made a nice save on Roope sliding across," Harley said.

The crowd cheered that stop and Hodges' second, sticking away a long-range puck on net from Tyler Seguin. Home fans were on his side even though Hodges played for the visiting team and the Stars needed to win to avoid facing the Western Conference top-seeded Colorado Avalanche in the first round of the playoffs.

Hodges had practiced plenty of times with Dallas and felt right at home.

"The blinders come on and you just see the ice ahead of you," he said. "Time seemed to travel pretty quickly. I knew my job was to go out there and do my absolute best, and I really tried. I really tried."

Trevor Zegras took an interference penalty almost midway through the period that put Dallas on the power play. Jason Robertson beat Hodges for a power-play goal to give Dallas the lead.

"[That] was an unlucky bounce for him," Harley said.

It was also the final shot the Ducks allowed the Stars to put on net. Hodges gloved down a dump-in later to more applause from the crowd.

The Ducks tried to tie it to get the game into overtime but couldn't crack Dallas goaltender Jake Oettinger, who was a perfect 9-of-9 on saves in the third period. The Stars added an empty-net goal to win 4–2, and Hodges became the first EBUG to get a loss in an NHL game.

That didn't stop him from being named third star of the game and getting a game puck for his efforts—two saves on three shots in the biggest pressure situation he'd ever faced in hockey.

Hodges was on the receiving end of fist bumps and hugs from not only Ducks players and coaches but Seguin and the rest of the Stars, who knew him from countless practice sessions.

"That's a great story," Stars coach Rick Bowness said. "I'm very happy for him."

––––––––––––

Hodges immediately became a hockey hero as the first EBUG to enter an NHL game since David Ayres on February 22, 2020, just before the start of the pandemic. He was out of breath by the time he did his first postgame TV interview and was still trying to comprehend the moment.

When he was done with his first media obligation, coaches told Hodges players were waiting for him in the locker room.

They showered him with water from bottles—the same treatment Ayres got in Toronto after his triumphant relief appearance more than two years earlier.

"I have nothing but positive things to say about the Ducks guys," Hodges said. "They played their hearts out for me, and I really tried to play my heart out for them. I know I did let in a goal. I did everything in my power to sort of help them win. We didn't. But I did my very best, so that's something that I'm very proud of."

Hodges was handed the game puck and asked to make a speech.

"Hey boys, thanks so much for having me tonight," he said in the middle of a jubilant locker room full of smiles. "I think everybody knows I was about ready to have a panic attack. But talking to you guys has made it so much easier. Thanks so much for calming me down."

Hodges' legend grew even more when he told reporters how he lost sight in his left eye and persevered to continue playing hockey.

"I've really spent a very long time trying not to be just the goalie with one eye," he said six days after his NHL appearance. "I'm so thankful to everybody involved for the opportunity of playing in the game."

After Hodges hit the showers, Nashville blew a 4–0 lead and lost to the Coyotes. The results of the night pushed the Stars into the second wild-card spot in the West and set up a matchup against Calgary and sent the Predators to Denver to face the high-powered Avalanche.

When the playoffs started a few days later, an injury to Pittsburgh Penguins goaltender Casey DeSmith in the second overtime of Game 1 of their series against the New York Rangers put the NHL on the verge of a potential EBUG situation. Reid Robertson was next in line to play at Madison Square Garden, but backup Louis Domingue stopped all 17 shots he faced, and the league did not get its first modern playoff EBUG.

Hodges could indeed be the last if rules are changed to allow each team to always carry a third goalie in some way. A week after playing for the Ducks and becoming an NHL player, he was still awaiting a nameplate he could attach to the jersey, which was hanging with others he had from other near misses with the Stars and Florida Panthers.

"It's all a little bit overwhelming, and I'm hoping that I've represented both the Stars and Anaheim well," he said.

His father had done the math just to show how rare this occasion was with just three emergency goalies getting into a game. Hodges joined the company of Ayres and Scott Foster, who were rooting for him when he went in.

Foster turned on the Ducks-Stars game when he heard about the latest EBUG. "Life is still cool sometimes," he said. Ayres kept hoping Anaheim would score to get Hodges the victory.

"At least he got in. I'm sure he was scared but loved it at the same time," Ayres said. "So happy he got in the game. Such an awesome experience for him."

It could take some time for Hodges to appreciate the moment. What immediately came to mind was his mother, who died two years earlier.

"It's been really tough," he said. "With a big life event like this, it's made it really tough. My dad still lives locally, and we're just trying to get by."

With his 15 minutes of fame over for now, Hodges was back to being a New York Life insurance salesman and had to take a phone call from his boss. Hockey was in his rearview mirror for the moment, but not forgotten.

"Experience of a lifetime," he said. "Something I'm going to remember for the rest of my life."

CHAPTER 9

GETTING THE CALL: SPECTACULAR TALES OF RUSHING TO THE RINK

THE FIRST TIME DAVID AYRES was called to be an emergency backup goaltender for a game, he was not even in the same country, let alone the same building.

Ayres called out sick from his job as building operator at Mattamy Athletic Center in Toronto because he wasn't feeling well. When Will Burns from the equipment staff of the American Hockey League's Toronto Marlies he practiced with regularly called to tell him to get his gear because he was needed in Rochester, New York, Ayres told him, "I feel like shit." He had also been pranked enough times before that he didn't think it was real. When Marlies general manager Kyle Dubas finally called and told him this was a real emergency, Ayres got out of bed, loaded his goaltending gear into his truck, and began the frantic trip from his home east of Toronto to Western New York.

Believing his Marlies jersey was at their home arena, Ricoh Coliseum, Ayres stopped there only to find out it was already in the travel trunk with the team. Having already wasted valuable time, he stepped on the gas.

"I was definitely beating the speed limit," he said. "I probably would've gotten pulled over four or five times if there was cops hanging around."

When Ayres got to the Canada–U.S. border, the guard asked where he was headed.

"I'm going to watch a hockey game," Ayres responded. He was sent off on his way. He worried that if he mentioned he was going to *play* in a game that he'd be asked to show paperwork and explain the situation. He didn't have time for that.

There was an accident near the Buffalo airport, so Ayres had to go the long way. He was worried he wouldn't make it on time.

"I was flying around neighborhoods and stuff just trying to get there," he said. "There was no way I was missing it. Even if I show up five minutes before warm-up, I was still doing it."

Ayres had lost some weight from the illness and was down from 210 pounds to 195. He was also pale in the face, but none of that mattered when he reached the arena a half-hour before warm-ups began and was able to dress in his first professional hockey game.

By the time Scott Foster got into his game in Chicago in 2018 and Ayres played for the Carolina Hurricanes against the Maple Leafs in 2020, he and the other emergency backup goaltenders around the NHL had to be standing by waiting in the arena with their gear. But in the previous two decades, a handful of other goalies got the call and rushed to the rink for a once-in-a-lifetime opportunity.

———

Chris Levesque was in the library at the University of British Columbia late in the morning of December 9, 2003, studying for the final exam in his geography class that was scheduled for the following morning. The 23-year-old UBC goaltender was immersed in that work and was wholly unaware Vancouver Canucks goaltender Dan Cloutier strained a groin muscle at the team's morning skate and would not be able to play in the game that night against the Pittsburgh Penguins.

At GM Place downtown, general manager Brian Burke and the Canucks were panicking because they needed a goalie to back up Johan Hedberg and couldn't get anyone from the minors to Vancouver on that short of notice. His staff knew a guy and reached out to coaches at UBC. No one could find or get ahold of Levesque.

Thunderbirds teammate Casey Bartzen finally tracked him down at the library. He grabbed Levesque and told him the Canucks needed him to suit up for their game.

"I don't have time for this," Levesque said. Bartzen pulled him out of his chair and gave him a phone number to call. Sure enough, it wasn't a cruel prank, and Levesque sprung into action.

Levesque had to get from the library on one side of UBC's campus to the rink on the other side to pick up his goaltending gear. And he couldn't exactly show up for an NHL game in the street clothes he was wearing to study, so he went to his off-campus home to change into a suit.

"It was pretty much grip it and rip it," he said.

Levesque hightailed it to the arena, was escorted to the place the players parked, and signed his one-day contract. By the time he made it to the Canucks locker room, players were already getting dressed for warm-ups.

He had skated with several players as part of workouts with local trainer Peter Twist, so the familiarity was there. He had also taken warm-ups plenty of times before at UBC, but that was in front of hundreds of people, if not a little more.

"It's not like we were packing the barn at UBC at the time," Levesque said. "Obviously it's a wee bit different being on the ice with that sort of crowd."

Levesque got to live out the dream of skating out before the game to U2's "Where the Streets Have No Name" with the rest of the Canucks and taking a seat. But that was just the beginning of his crazy night.

Tom Fenton was preparing to visit his parents back home in Sarnia, Ontario, and wanted to look presentable for his mother. So, he went to the SuperCuts in White Plains, New York, to get a haircut on the afternoon of December 16, 2010.

Fenton was a graduate assistant in the athletic department at Manhattanville College in Purchase, New York, and was a full season removed from playing goal at American International College. His youth and junior hockey experience took him from Sarnia to Petrolia, where his goalie partner in 2001–02 was Foster, and on to Milton, Ontario. The opportunity to play Division I hockey took him to AIC in Springfield, Massachusetts, but after four rough years there, Fenton passed up the opportunity to play in a league in the United Kingdom and didn't want to bounce around Europe or become a career minor leaguer in the low levels across North America.

"I wanted to get my professional life going, and I knew the statistics around getting to the NHL," he said. "I didn't know if I wanted to go play in the ECHL. I didn't know if I'd even get that opportunity. I thought I'd be like a Central [Hockey] League goalie or go take my chances in Europe, so I wanted to slowly get out of the game."

As part of his grad assistant job, Fenton was a goaltending coach for the Manhattanville men's and women's hockey teams.

The 26-year-old was also making some extra money on the side coaching youth hockey goalies with the Rye Rangers program.

While sitting in the barber chair at SuperCuts, Fenton felt his phone continue to buzz in his pocket. Not wanting to ruin his haircut ahead of the visit home, he ignored it at first. But the buzzing didn't stop, so he checked his phone and saw several calls from a number he didn't recognize and one from Rye Rangers coach Steve Ketchabaw. He called Ketchabaw back.

"Pick up your fucking phone," Ketchabaw said. "The GM of the Phoenix Coyotes is going to call you. They want you to suit up and play."

Ilya Bryzgalov had started for the Coyotes the previous night at the New Jersey Devils, but he came down with the flu and wasn't able to dress for their game at Madison Square Garden against the New York Rangers. Jason LaBarbera was in line to start, but the Coyotes desperately needed a backup. Because goaltending coach Sean Burke was a retired NHL professional at the position, rules at the time stated he'd need to clear waivers and that would take 24 hours the team didn't have. Video coordinator Steve Peters was a backup goalie at the University of North Dakota a couple of decades earlier, but the Coyotes needed him to do his job during the game.

The Coyotes called Fenton and asked if he would do them a favor by coming down to the arena. He said yes without hesitation, then realized everything he'd need to do to get from Manhattanville College to downtown Manhattan by 5 PM. Add to the complications that Fenton's truck was having problems, so he asked good friend David Turco to borrow his SUV for the drive. Turco agreed.

"He's my boy," Fenton said. "He knew what was going on. He's a hockey guy. He thought the story was great. He just wanted me to get him tickets."

Fenton hadn't put on his gear in at least a month and hadn't played a competitive game since March 7, 2009, against Holy Cross while at AIC. He knew it was stored at the PlayLand rink in Rye and rushed to get there and pick it up. But that was no match for the drive into New York that he was able to cut good chunks of time off to make it through traffic and get there on time.

"It was chaos," Fenton said. "Probably driving too fast, cutting too many people off."

On the way, Fenton called as many friends and family members as he could to tell them what was happening. Maybe half of them actually believed him. He told his parents to make sure they put the Coyotes–Rangers game on at their place.

Fenton reached Madison Square Garden and paid $40 in cash to park across the street. For a graduate assistant who wasn't making a lot, that was good beer money out of his pocket. But he made it and knew someone working for the Rangers who helped him get into the building. He was greeted by retired NHL defenseman-turned-assistant Ulf Samuelsson and received a wave of thanks from Coyotes players and coaches.

"I was in awe and kind of a little bit starstruck the whole time," he said.

Defenseman Keith Yandle and forward Vernon Fiddler insisted on taking Fenton's picture when he signed his one-day amateur tryout contract. He took a physical before the game, and, despite keeping himself in shape, heard plenty of jokes from Coyotes players: "*This guy* is suiting up with us?"

Fenton caught plenty of flak from veteran Derek Morris for his bright yellow goalie stick from his time with the AIC Yellow Jackets. Morris told him, "You're not using those," so Fenton grabbed one of the other sticks lying around to take warm-ups and took his place as the backup goaltender on the bench while LaBarbera faced the Rangers.

"Can you imagine if LaBarbera gets hurt in any way?" color analyst Joe Micheletti said on the New York broadcast on MSG. "And you don't want to see it, of course."

Fenton did a TV interview at each intermission. LaBarbera played the entire game and the Coyotes lost 4–3 in a shootout. Captain Shane Doan tried to talk referees Dave Jackson and Justin St-Pierre into giving Fenton a phantom penalty to get him on the scoresheet. Jackson told him the days of doing that were long gone, unless Fenton unloaded a series of F-bombs from the bench. He was not about to do anything like that in his first and only NHL game.

LaBarbera wanted Fenton to join him for dinner and a drink in New York, but the exhaustion of the day—even with zero minutes of game action—took a toll.

Fenton declined, choosing instead to go home and have a couple of beers with two buddies and relax before his flight the next day.

"I was just mentally exhausted," he said. "I had some long games, triple-overtime games growing up, things like that, long games in college, but just doing that drive and everything that was going on, I was just mentally wiped out."

Fenton's drive home came at a much more leisurely pace. He left the lot he had rushed into not the least bit worried about the Coyotes paying him back for his $40 in parking.

"They don't owe me anything," he said.

———

Several years later, the team was known as the Arizona Coyotes but was again in need of an emergency backup goaltender, this time for a home game February 15, 2016, against the Montreal Canadiens after Anders Lindback ruptured an Achilles tendon.

Naturally, their call went to a financial adviser who played club hockey at Arizona State and was a son of a former Coyotes coach.

Nathan Schoenfeld grew up around hockey because his father, Jim, was coaching in the NHL from the late 1980s through the '90s. During Jim Schoenfeld's days coaching the New Jersey Devils, his kids Justin, Kate, Adam, and Nathan were constantly around the practice facility. By the time he moved on to the Washington Capitals, it was down to his two youngest, Adam and Nathan.

While at the Piney Orchard Ice Arena in Odenton, Maryland, young Nathan Schoenfeld gravitated toward the goaltenders. He loved Don Beaupre's red-white-and-blue mask and became a fan of Capitals netminders Jim Carey and Olie Kolzig. Carey won the Vezina Trophy as the league's top goaltender in 1996.

Schoenfeld was already a fan of future Hall of Famer Patrick Roy after watching every game of the Montreal Canadiens Stanley Cup run in 1993. His dad was not coaching at the time and had taken a TV analyst position, so Nathan was free to pick his own team to root for outside of family ties.

He played hockey as a skater growing up until his team lost a few close games. Schoenfeld thought, *I'd rather be the goalie and have the opportunity to win that game instead of losing it. I can get us over the hump.* After one season splitting his time, Schoenfeld became a full-time goaltender and never looked back.

By the time his dad coached the Coyotes from 1997–99, Nathan was a teenager and too old to hang out around the rink like he used to do. That was a safe space for players to complain about their coach demoting or scratching them. Little did he know that he'd be back in that locker room almost two decades later.

Schoenfeld played competitively throughout high school and could see where his goaltending career was going, so he didn't make much of an effort to advance it beyond that. After playing with Adam in high school, Nathan wanted to continue that in college. They played club hockey at Arizona State, making nationals one season, and Nathan raved about the quality of the play at that level.

"It was a perfect avenue," Schoenfeld said. "It was a great way to still be around hockey and enjoy it. Obviously, you're not at the NCAA level, but it was still competitive and hard games."

He graduated from Arizona State with a finance degree in 2006 and went into the mortgage industry before doing some financial advising. Schoenfeld advanced in the business world, got married, and his wife, Colby, gave birth to the couple's first child, Kesler, in 2013. Twin boys Rhett and Drake were born in early 2016.

Because it was Presidents' Day and banks were closed, Schoenfeld was home from work. The five-week-old boys had a little cough, so he and Colby had them in the bath. Nathan was also trying to play with two-and-a-half-year-old Kesler, so they were running around the house when he got the text message from father-in-law and Coyotes head equipment manager Stan Wilson: "Hey, we may need you tonight."

It was after 6 PM, and the game was scheduled to start in an hour. Schoenfeld stared at his phone, told his wife, and responded asking if this was real. Wilson said he'd double-check, and the two traded a handful of messages over the next three or four minutes. Yes, Wilson said, Lindback was injured off the ice getting ready for the game and the team needed someone to back up Louis Domingue.

Schoenfeld had zero margin for error and rushed around collecting all his gear. He made sure Colby was set with the kids and double- and triple-checked his hockey bag. Kesler watched with confusion as his dad made sure he didn't forget anything.

"It was just a mad scramble to make sure I had what I needed," Schoenfeld said. "It was chaotic. The heart's racing, a little bit of butterflies starting already."

He said his goodbyes, flew out the door, and, like Fenton six years earlier, called everyone he could think of. He called his mom, dad, and siblings to tell him he was on the way to dress for the Coyotes in an NHL game. That didn't exactly slow him down on the 25-minute trip to the arena in Glendale. There was a bit of zig-zagging, but Schoenfeld didn't have to break any laws to make it.

"I was cruising pretty good down the highway trying to get there in time," he said. "It was definitely a crazy 45 minutes."

When he arrived, a cart was set up for him to throw his gear on. Schoenfeld rushed in and signed his amateur tryout contract. By the time he got to the locker room, Arizona players were coming off the ice from warm-ups that they had gone through with just one goalie.

During his frantic rush out of the house and to the rink, Schoenfeld did not have much time to think. The nerves came when he was getting dressed in the locker room. He tried to remember the order to put things on, and his hands were shaking as he tied his skates. Good friend and Coyotes forward Max Domi gave him a high-five, and Wilson walked over to tell Schoenfeld to relax and take his time.

Unlike the rest of his teammates that night, Schoenfeld didn't get any kind of a warm-up. He did not have a puck shot at him any time while in uniform. But he made sure to skate a lap around the ice when the Coyotes came out before the national anthems to take a look around the arena—"Just enough to say I was on the ice."

The amazement lasted throughout the game, watching Montreal's P.K. Subban patrol the blue line and marveling at the speed of the play from ice level.

Things went well on the ice for the Coyotes. Domingue stopped 17 of the 19 shots he faced, six different players scored a goal, and Arizona won 6–2. Schoenfeld was in the thick of the excitement on the bench. The nerves settled down as the game went on.

"I don't think in my mind I ever thought I was going in, so maybe that helped," he said. "But it was a fun bench to be on."

After the final horn sounded, Schoenfeld's focus was on getting Kesler to the locker room for pictures in his No. 40 Coyotes jersey. His mind drifted there, but the team had a tradition after victories of handing out a championship belt. He was surprised when Doan handed it to him.

"It was the icing on the cake," said Schoenfeld, who then mustered up a little speech for the boys about the thrill of the night. In true hockey player fashion, he pivoted to the big win and two valuable points for the Coyotes.

Schoenfeld was joined by his eldest son. They got pictures with him in uniform and holding the belt.

"I just couldn't stop smiling," he said.

When Schoenfeld got around to checking his phone, there were more than 200 unread text messages. Family members in Canada were sending him tweets and mentions on TSN and Sportsnet.

He got messages and calls at work the next day and for the next two-plus weeks from news outlets wanting to do a story on him.

"It was crazy," he said.

The story still comes up years later. At the rink one day, his sons' skating coach during a chat brought it up. "You were the goalie, right?"

"It's just funny that it still gets brought up years later, that people recognize it," Schoenfeld said. "I thought it was something that would happen to me and we would never hear about it again, but it's a story that just lives on."

———————————

Eric Semborski was running a children's learn-to-skate class at Flyers Skate Zone in Voorhees, New Jersey, on the morning of December 3, 2016, with no knowledge that the Chicago Black-hawks were scrambling on the other side of the Delaware River in Philadelphia. Goaltender Corey Crawford had an emergency appendectomy, and they needed someone to back up Scott Dar-ling for their afternoon game at the Flyers.

The Blackhawks couldn't use goalie coach Jimmy Waite because he had played in the NHL, and they were up against the salary cap. He'd count as a professional, so the Blackhawks needed an amateur. They reached out to the Flyers for local options. Semborski played pickup games at Wells Fargo Center with team employees and was known to the front office from that and his day job.

When Semborski stepped off the ice at the rink that doubles as the Flyers practice facility, assistant general manager Barry Hanrahan asked him a handful of questions about his playing history and other hockey experience. The native of Bloomsburg, Pennsylvania, told Hanrahan he played club hockey at Temple University for four seasons. Hanrahan typed the answers into his phone, and Semborski asked what the line of questioning was all about. Hanrahan told him the Blackhawks were looking for a goaltender and would call if they needed him. Semborski needed to rush home to his place in the Manayunk section of Philadelphia to get his gear before making his way to the arena in South Philly.

Puck drop was two hours away, so Semborski did not have much time to spare. On his way, he got a call from a Chicago number and confirmed he was on his way. After his frantic interstate drive, Semborski rolled down the tunnel to the players' parking lot and entered Wells Fargo Center. He signed his amateur tryout contract in the coaches' room and made his way to the visiting locker room.

Semborski arrived to find Crawford's No. 50 jersey with his nameplate on it hanging in a locker stall with the rest of his gear. Blackhawks players erupted in a round of applause after getting a goalie there with time to spare. Of course, they gave him a hard time for being late, but the best hockey of Semborski's life was still ahead—as was his brief chance to stand in the crease during an NHL game.

CHAPTER 10

AMONG THE STARS:
NHL SPOTLIGHT IS BRIGHT
FROM WARM-UPS ON

EMERGENCY BACKUP GOALTENDERS around the NHL have the debate: Would you rather dress for a game and just sit on the bench, or get called in to go on the ice for a practice and face live shots?

Several have gotten the best of both worlds by taking part in pregame warm-ups. Of course, the dream is going in for game action like Scott Foster, David Ayres, and Tom Hodges, but the chance to warm up on NHL ice in front of fans is the next best thing. It's also something Foster, Ayres, and Hodges didn't get to do before they went in.

———

Brett Leonhardt became a goaltender because he liked the attention. He doesn't think he's alone in that.

"Anyone who plays net who doesn't tell you that is lying," he said. "It was the one position in hockey that was different, just like a pitcher in baseball."

His older brother was also goalie, so Leonhardt had the hand-me-down equipment to use when he got his turn in net. The country kid went to the "big city" of Kitchener, Ontario, to play youth hockey starting at age eight and advanced through minor hockey while being an average-sized goaltender. He had his biggest growth spurt in 1998 when he went to under-17 camp for Team Ontario, discovering he had grown from 5'10" to 6'3" in one year.

Leonhardt played junior hockey in Cambridge and Kitchener from ages 17–21. He feared his goaltending career was over because playing in a couple of Ontario Hockey League exhibition games ruined his eligibility to play Division I college hockey in the United States.

"I was ready to just quit hockey," Leonhardt said.

He was sold on going to Oswego State University for the next best thing, Division III, and played against the likes of Keith Aucoin during his time there from 2003 to '05. He transferred to Neumann College and played two more seasons before reaching the NHL—as web producer for the Washington Capitals.

Now 6'7", 26 years old, and nicknamed "Stretch," Leonhardt got plenty of on-ice work as a Capitals practice goalie when Olie Kolzig and Jose Theodore wanted a break. When Theodore was sore on December 12, 2008, Leonhardt filled in as the second goalie with Brent Johnson at the morning skate and thought little of it.

Behind the scenes at the Capitals practice facility, general manager George McPhee and staffers learned that Theodore was banged up worse than they thought. Someone joked that the team might have to use Stretch that night against the Ottawa Senators. After a couple of laughs, they realized it was a possibility.

Top goalie prospect Semyon Varlamov was on a rare Texas road trip with the American Hockey League's Hershey Bears, who were bussing from San Antonio to Houston. The other choice was Michal Neuvirth, who was on the Gulf Coast of Florida with the ECHL's South Carolina Stingrays. The Capitals worked to get Varlamov to Washington, but it wasn't going to be easy.

The Capitals called Hershey coach Bob Woods and told him Varlamov was getting called up and had a 1 PM local time flight out of Houston. The Bears were almost three hours away, and broadcaster John Walton said to Woods, "If we had a rocket launcher on the back of this bus, we're not going to be in Houston at 1 o'clock." That timing wasn't going to work, so Woods called back, and the Capitals put Varlamov on the next possible flight.

When the bus pulled up to a gas station in Gonzales, Texas, Varlamov and his gear were unloaded so he could get in another car and make it to the airport on time. He was headed to the NHL complete with a message from Alex Ovechkin welcoming him, but no one was sure when Varlamov would make it.

Leonhardt was the backup plan, even if he didn't know it yet. He got his first inkling when goaltending coach Dave Prior sought him out to tell him to get some rest during the afternoon. McPhee pulled Leonhardt into his office to bring him up to speed—the Capitals were trying to bring in another goalie for the game, but they needed a fallback plan. Leonhardt would only fit the bill if he never played professional hockey. When he confirmed he hadn't, he was told to get ready.

"I didn't go home," Leonhardt said. "I was so nervous, and I didn't know what was going on."

At 3 PM, McPhee delivered the message: "You're going tonight." Leonhardt signed his one-day contract with assistant GM Don Fishman and prepared for warm-ups.

Leonhardt had taken shots from Alex Ovechkin, Nicklas Backstrom, Mike Green, and future Hall of Famer Sergei Fedorov plenty of times in practice. But this was on a Friday night in full uniform at an NHL arena with the spotlight on him.

"The warm-up for me though is the hardest part because you're being taped," he said. "It's going to be all over the news. So you got to look like you've been there before and try to be competitive."

Can't get much more attention than that.

Buzz built up throughout the day that something was off and Leonhardt would at least start in uniform, but the Capitals didn't announce anything until he jumped on for warm-ups. Media relations director Nate Ewell walked around the press box informing everyone that the tall goalie on the ice was Leonhardt.

"It wasn't anything to brag about," Ewell said. "But then I had to spread the word."

Leonhardt was having the time of his life. For a moment, he felt like a nervous kid fresh out of college, and then the routine settled him down.

"It's funny, like the NHL, 'Oh my god,' right, but once you go out there and get into it, you do the same warm-up in junior, in college," he said. "It was pretty relaxed and kind of a cool environment and kind of forced you to calm your nerves and do what you'd done your whole life."

Watching from high above the ice, Ewell was nervous but excited that a coworker was getting this unprecedented opportunity. By the time the Bears got to Houston, they heard that Leonhardt was backing up. *Whoa*, Walton thought. *That escalated quickly.*

Leonhardt took his place on the bench as Johnson's backup and was there for just over nine minutes of game time before Varlamov showed up and sent the web producer back to his full-time job. After the Capitals' 5–1 win, Leonhardt held court in the locker room with media members and filmed players doing their scrums while still in his goalie pads.

That was good practice for his second EBUG scare November 29, 2013. Michal Neuvirth was injured during warm-ups, so Leonhardt got dressed and in uniform and was listed as Braden Holtby's backup. But Leonhardt had become video coach at this point, so he did that job with some gear on. Washington beat Montreal 3–2 in a shootout to improve to a perfect 2-0-0 with Leonhardt in uniform.

Ten years after his on-ice cameo, Leonhardt's name was engraved on the Stanley Cup for his video-coaching role in the Capitals winning it all in 2018.

Unlike Foster, whom he played with for a season in Petrolia, Tom Fenton did not want to keep playing hockey regularly after college.

"I wasn't one of these goalies that continuously wanted to get pucks shot at my head for years after," he said.

Fenton had not put the pads on for at least a month in his role as goaltending coach for Manhattanville College's men's and women's teams. He hadn't played competitively in 21 months since his last game at American International College and wasn't sure if the Coyotes knew that when they called him in to dress for them at the New York Rangers on December 16, 2010.

"That's the scary part," he said. "I was still in shape because I was just out of college and I was still taking care of myself and on the ice every day in some component, but I wasn't taking pucks."

The chance to dust off his equipment and feel pucks again came in pregame warm-ups at Madison Square Garden. Fenton took a lap around the rink at the "World's Most Famous Arena" and looked over to see the Rangers with Marian Gaborik, Chris Drury, Sean Avery, and, of course, Henrik Lundqvist in his prime. He skated by them, stopped at center ice, and looked straight up at the iconic videoboard.

What the hell? Fenton thought. *What am I doing here? Holy crap; I'm in an NHL game.*

Fenton spent the Coyotes–Rangers game on the bench while Jason LaBarbera started, but he certainly had a different feeling about the Madison Square Garden ice than some NHL players who aren't big fans. When he stepped off, he mentioned to the rink crew that he thought the ice was great—especially compared to where he was used to skating.

"These guys were so happy that I said that," he said. "I got the biggest grin I ever received from the Zamboni driver."

———

Thirteen years after the Vancouver Canucks used Chris Levesque as their backup goaltender and more than five years since Jordan White dressed for the San Jose Sharks against his hometown team, another University of British Columbia goaltender got the call to dress in the NHL on October 18, 2016.

This time it was Matt Hewitt, a 23-year-old from nearby Westminster who played three years with the Western Hockey League's Regina Pats and was heading into his fourth season at UBC. Projected starter Ryan Miller was ruled out for the game against the St. Louis Blues that night with tightness, and the Canucks needed someone to back up Jacob Markstrom. While trying to sleep in at his parents' house, Hewitt missed multiple calls from his coach and woke up to voicemail messages telling him, "You're going up to play in the big leagues."

"I kind of just woke up not knowing anything," Hewitt said. "All of a sudden here I am, I've got to get ready to gear up for the Canucks."

The rest of the day felt like a dream for Hewitt, no time more so than pregame warm-ups. After growing up watching Daniel and Henrik Sedin, they were passing the puck in rapid succession, stickhandling, and messing around with him—while wearing the same uniform.

"It was fun being in net as those guys shoot on me," Hewitt said.

He instantly saw and felt the difference of facing NHL shooters compared to those in university or even WHL games. The almost 20 minutes on the ice flew by.

"It did go really fast and you're just trying to find your spot on the ice and not trying to get in the way of anybody and their routines," he said. "I just tried to take in the moment and just embrace my opportunity when I was in the net because I knew it wasn't going to be long-lived."

When he wasn't in net, Hewitt got to chat with Blues goaltender Carter Hutton, who spent his one game in uniform as an emergency backup six years earlier with the Philadelphia Flyers.

Hewitt hoped to follow Hutton's path from EBUG to the NHL, but it did not work out that way. He played two more seasons at UBC, putting up a .920 save percentage in the 2017–18 regular season and a .915 in three playoff games. Hockey took him to the Australian Ice Hockey League, where he played for a team in Canberra. He had stellar numbers for CBR Brave—a 1.95 goals-against average and .925 save percentage—and that earned him a job in 2018–19 in Italy with HC Fassa of the Alps Hockey League.

"I was playing in the Alps, and it was beautiful," he said.

While playing in the alpine resort town of Canazei, Hewitt received a call from Malcolm Cameron, an assistant from his time with Regina who was now coaching the ECHL's Wichita Thunder. Wichita was struggling to find someone to spell starter

Stuart Skinner, and Hewitt thought it was the next step in his goaltending career.

Instead, the Thunder scuffled down the stretch and Hewitt did not get any starts. When he was thrown in cold in relief twice, he allowed a total of seven goals on 45 shots.

"It didn't go so well during those games," Hewitt said. "We were also on a little bit of a losing streak, so it was a little bit frustrating. Then I ended up getting a concussion, so it shows you there can be a lot of highs and lows to hockey. Even though I do appreciate the experience and I'm grateful for it, it didn't turn out the way I wanted it to and that was unfortunate."

Hewitt almost wished he had stayed in Italy, where he had a good situation. The concussion with Wichita on a one-timer in practice was a stroke of bad fortune, though he made sure to prioritize his health over hockey at a time that he was not getting much playing time, anyway.

That season was the end of his goaltending career, and Hewitt moved to Lillooet, British Columbia, to become a wildland firefighter. The summer of 2021 proved to be a busy one for Hewitt, who began to enjoy the camaraderie of working on a crew of 20.

"It was nice to be in that team environment again where you're working with others," he said. "So, I kind of felt close to home with myself."

Eric Semborski didn't get a lot of time to consider himself a member of the Chicago Blackhawks for a day before going out for warm-ups with them on December 3, 2016, in Philadelphia. After players introduced themselves in the visiting locker room at Wells Fargo Center, they truly welcomed him to the team on the ice.

When Semborski replaced Darling in the net for the first time during warm-ups, he got three easy shots. Then the surrounding Blackhawks players glanced around at each other, smiled, and opened fire on the unsuspecting emergency backup goalie.

"They started picking me apart," Semborski said on *The Comcast Network* at the time. "It took me a little bit to try to catch up to that speed, but it was wild to see those shots from that perspective of them coming at you."

Semborski faced shots from the likes of Patrick Kane, Artemi Panarin, and future Hall of Famer Marian Hossa that afternoon. Once he adjusted to how quickly the shots were coming at him, Semborski settled in and made some solid saves.

"That was the best hockey I've ever played in my life," he said.

Semborski grew an appreciation that day for how NHL players release the puck and can be deceptive about when a shot is coming off the stick blade. By the end of the warm-up, his confidence was high—and then he was reminded of where he was.

"They put me in right at the end of warm-ups again when the goalie's kind of against the whole team and they're just trying to bang in the rebounds," Semborski said. "I made two saves and then they just roofed it bar down."

Late in the third period, Darling went to the bench for an extra attacker with Chicago down 3–1. Coaches told Semborski afterward that he would have gone into the game if the Flyers scored an empty-net goal to put the game out of reach. It turned out to be the second closest Semborski came to entering an NHL game in Philadelphia.

———

Cam Janssen likes to tell Tyler Stewart they're the two guys to make it to the NHL from Eureka High School in suburban St.

Louis. Janssen played in 346 games with the Blues and New Jersey Devils. Stewart's total? Zero, with one memorable pregame warm-up.

Early in his time playing club hockey at Saint Louis University, Stewart was invited to skate with Blues players who needed a goalie around for informal workouts during the 2012–13 NHL lockout that shortened the season to 48 games. Saint Louis alum Sean Ferrell, who was helping out at those skates, hooked on with the Blues as video coach the following season.

Stewart played in college until 2015 but was fed up with playing in beer leagues "because as a goalie you just get shelled, and everyone else thinks they can drink and just show up." Just when he was ready to call it quits in the fall of 2017, he got a call from Blues executive Ryan Miller. The NHL had instituted new emergency backup rules, so future Hall of Famer Martin Brodeur could no longer serve in the job for St. Louis while working in the front office and the team needed someone who had not played anywhere professionally.

Stewart was offered tickets, but he didn't need them because his family already had season tickets in section 313. No problem, Miller said, the team would comp those. The 25-year-old vending machine worker had only one request.

"The only thing I ask is maybe if you can get me parking passes," Stewart said, "because it's really hard to carry all that stuff miles away to the rink."

Easy enough, so Stewart took the gig. Growing up, he always wanted to work in hockey, but after interning with the Blues and getting a feel for the hours, workload, and stress, he decided it wasn't for him.

When the team contracted him to be an EBUG, he was fortunate enough to be working for his father, Scott, at Cardinal Vending, the family business his grandfather started in 1987. It was never a problem for Tyler to take a break from work when the Blues asked him to skate. His dad said to him, "You never know when it's going to be the last time."

Stewart skated with Blues players enough to wonder what it would be like to get into a game. Longtime defenseman Joel Edmundson once told him, "If you ever got in, Stewie, we'd play Game 7 defense for you." Edmundson did that for real, helping the Blues win the Stanley Cup in 2019 and again for Ayres with the Carolina Hurricanes less than a year later.

Stewart didn't get as far as Ayres, but on December 7, 2017, he became the first player since the NHL required emergency backup goaltenders to be in the building to dress for pregame warm-ups.

He went to work at 5 AM and was home hanging out with his wife and dog after his shift was over when he got the call. Carter Hutton took a puck off the foot during the morning skate and wouldn't be able to dress against the Dallas Stars. Like the Capitals nine years earlier with Varlamov, the Blues were trying to get Ville Husso in from San Antonio, but they couldn't confirm when he'd arrive and needed another goalie to take warm-ups with Jake Allen. Also like Leonhardt's situation in 2008, Stewart was told to keep it quiet and only told family members so they could make arrangements to attend the game.

Stewart got his "welcome to the NHL" moment while texting on his phone in the locker room to direct his parents where to pick up their tickets.

"Hey, put your phone away!" star winger Vladimir Tarasenko said. Stewart didn't know the team rule, and for the night he was part of the team.

Stewart doesn't remember hearing the iconic "When the Saints Go Marching In" on the arena organ when he stepped onto the ice for warm-ups because it was all a blur. Years later, he realizes he was too paranoid about messing up other players' routines to soak it in, but there were still plenty of memorable moments. He watched smooth-skating defenseman Jay Bouwmeester wheel around the ice going forward and backward and chatted with winger Scottie Upshall about Lululemon.

"Let's go, Stewie," Edmundson said as he gave Stewart a tap on the pads. Veteran alternate captain Alex Steen chatted him up. All of it was recorded from the stands in the form of photos and videos.

"The most random things were happening," Stewart recalled. "It was the fastest 15, 17 minutes ever."

Stewart had a job to do, too, and told Allen to let him know when the full-time NHL goalie wanted his temporary understudy to go in net and face some shots. "I'll stay out of your way," Stewart told Allen.

The moment really hit Stewart when he looked across the ice and saw Stars goalie and fellow St. Louis native Mike McKenna. The other NHL goaltender the area had produced was Ben Bishop, but he was scratched for Dallas that day.

Stewart got a picture with McKenna at the center red line, went back to the locker room after warm-ups, and marveled at Allen changing out of all his undergarments for dry clothing in the brief break before going back out for the game. Stewart was told to hang back in the locker room rather than join the rest of the Blues on the bench, and Husso was close enough to be listed as St. Louis' backup on the official roster sheet.

Husso got a police escort on the highway to get from the airport to the arena, thanked Stewart when he arrived, and got dressed to take his place on the bench during the first period. Like Bishop, Stewart was scratched. He did some interviews and was given a couple of game pucks. Allen made 29 saves to shut out the Stars in a 3–0 Blues victory, and Stewart left the rink smiling.

"It was so cool to be out there with the guys," Stewart said. "A storybook ending except I didn't get to play."

Neither of Gavin McHale's parents played hockey. His father was born in England, and his mother grew up without much of anything.

He got his introduction to the sport playing mini sticks in the basement with friends.

Once he tried playing on the ice, he realized he wasn't a good player.

"When the opportunity to play goalie came up, I'd been doing that for years in the basement and in street hockey and stuff," McHale said. "So, I jumped at it, and I was really good so I just kind of stuck with it."

McHale stuck with it through the Manitoba Junior Hockey League, playing with the Portage Terriers, and advanced at age 17 to play two seasons of major junior hockey in the Western Hockey League with the Seattle Thunderbirds and Lethbridge Hurricanes.

His career started taking twists in 2016 with stints in the British Columbia Hockey League, Alberta Junior Hockey League, and Manitoba Junior Hockey League. After two years at the University of Manitoba, he kept his career going in the Manitoba East Hockey League and South Eastern Manitoba Hockey League through 2015.

Three years later, he was skating with the defending Stanley Cup champions.

Leonhardt said he would have been overcome with nerves to take shots from Ovechkin and Backstrom if he didn't know and practice with them already. So, naturally, he could feel for McHale 10 years later in Winnipeg.

Braden Holtby was battling an injury, but the Capitals did not know until hours before their game at the Jets that he would not be able to back up Pheonix Copley. McHale—also 6'7" like Leonhardt, who as a team employee was no longer eligible to dress—was in line to be the emergency backup goaltender that night.

McHale, 31, was wrapping up practice as goalie coach of the University of Manitoba women's hockey team at 5:15 PM when he had a series of text messages and a missed call from Capitals goaltending coach Scott Murray. He was needed right away.

Planning to drive with his mother to the game, he instead met up with her in the parking lot of Polo Park shopping center and told her he was dressing for Washington. They couldn't reach his father because he always went out to pick up sushi when he would be watching the game by himself on TV. McHale weaved through traffic to get to the arena and got ahold of his dad just as he was about to park. He got to see his girlfriend briefly, too, before getting to work.

McHale had a white No. 41 Capitals jersey with his name on it waiting in the visiting locker room. There was no time to eat dinner between the time he got the call and stepped on the ice for warm-ups.

A strength and conditioning coach who also oversaw goalies for a local junior team in addition to his duties at the University of Manitoba, he was starstruck. The first shot he saw in warm-ups came from Ovechkin.

It went in the net.

"Not even close," McHale told reporters afterward. "I was pretty starstruck. It was like, 'Who's shooting on me now?' Probably should have been focusing a little more on the puck."

In a Capitals uniform taking shots from the defending Stanley Cup champions, McHale served as target practice for 2014 Sochi Olympics U.S. star T.J. Oshie to work on his shootout moves. His parents, Ian and Vale, watched from high above the ice. His mother told The Canadian Press that night, "This is his dream come true to go on the surface in an NHL game."

Normalcy returned for McHale while sitting by himself along the glass during the game—the only room for the backup goalie at the arena in Winnipeg because the benches are too small. Washington coach Todd Reirden was glad Copley played the entire game and didn't have to go to the backup. He was happy to have McHale around.

"He was fine in the warm-up," Reirden said. "It was a great opportunity for a local guy. As we've seen in the league over the last couple of years, you never know. He was great coming into our room and talking to our guys."

It wasn't McHale's first time in an NHL uniform. Six weeks before Foster played for the Blackhawks against the Jets, McHale was the emergency backup in Winnipeg on February 16, 2018, when Colorado goaltender Jonathan Bernier took a puck off the mask and gave way to Varlamov for the third period. McHale got a tap on the shoulder while watching from the press box, rushed down to the visiting locker room, and put on his gear and an Avalanche jersey with the No. 61 on it.

While McHale didn't get to keep that jersey, he got his from the night with Washington along with a custom stall tag with his name on it as part of an entire swag bag from the Capitals. After a rushed experience with the Avalanche, McHale got to enjoy this one more.

"I got to dress with the team and kind of be in the room throughout the game and stuff," he said years later. "It's not lost on me how lucky I am that I got that opportunity."

After Ovechkin delivered an autographed stick. Holtby came over with one, too, and struck up a conversation with McHale at the locker stall that should have been his.

McHale played junior hockey in Holtby's hometown of Lloydminster on the border of Saskatchewan and Alberta. McHale said on NHL Network the next day, "We chatted about the good old days in Lloydminster. I knew it was probably my last chance to take his stall."

McHale continued serving as an EBUG in Winnipeg through February 2020. He still works with the University of Manitoba women's team and runs Maverick Coaching Academy, helping fitness professionals build their businesses.

Throughout the game appearances by Foster and Ayres, McHale remained the last emergency backup goaltender to take part in warm-ups until early in the 2021 season.

University of Toronto goalie Alex Bishop got that opportunity with the Toronto Maple Leafs after learning the night before that they needed him for at least the morning skate. The skate itself gave Bishop the chance to take shots 1-on-1 from Auston Matthews while the NHL's reigning top goal-scorer worked his way back from wrist surgery.

By the time he was on the ice for warm-ups getting shots from the likes of Mitch Marner, John Tavares, and William Nylander, Bishop felt comfortable in net.

"At the end of the day, it's just hockey, right?" he said. "You're a goalie. You're just there to stop the puck."

It was everything else around stopping the puck that over-whelmed Bishop. He tried to keep from getting distracted by the spotlight or bumping into Maple Leafs players.

"You never really see how loud it is or how bright it is until you're right down there at ice level," he said. "I don't even really know how to explain it. I came on the ice, and you see all the flashing cameras and everything and obviously that's not something you experience in university hockey—people on the boards, people with signs and asking for pucks and sticks and everything."

Less than two months later, Bishop got to be one of those fans banging on the glass when University of Toronto teammate and housemate Jett Alexander took warm-ups at the same arena with the visiting Colorado Avalanche. Like Stewart, Alexander was a stand-in until a goalie could get there from the minors, and when Justus Annunen made it in time, he watched the game from the stands with his girlfriend, Bishop, and some other teammates.

Alexander got to brag about not allowing a goal in warm-ups, even though plenty of guys missed the net while he was in there.

"I guess you could say you were forcing guys there," Alexander joked. "Pucks were just coming off their sticks so hard I couldn't really keep up to them."

It wasn't lost on Alexander that he was on the ice with Colorado stars Nathan MacKinnon, Mikko Rantanen, Gabriel Landeskog, and Cale Makar. This was certainly not a warm-up before a university game.

"Guys shoot the puck harder and can zap the puck around a bit quicker and everything, and you can tell they think the game faster," he said. "But it's obviously a big step and once you get there, you're like, 'Wow.'"

Alexander wasn't worried about getting scored on or if any of the Avalanche players even knew who he was. They at least knew his last name from the back of his Colorado jersey, which he hung up in his room shortly after.

"It's something that not many people get to do in their lives, so something I'll be able to talk about and tell that story while having a beer down the road," Alexander said.

The same goes for Kyle Konin, who took warm-ups and backed up for the Blues at the Tampa Bay Lightning on December 2, 2021, one night after Alexander's game in Toronto. Konin's claim to fame during warm-ups at Amalie Arena was the solo lap St. Louis players made him take without his helmet on.

CHAPTER 11

CLOSE CALLS: THE TIMES AN EMERGENCY BACKUP WAS ALMOST NEEDED

B EFORE COLLIN DELIA'S severe leg cramping opened the door for Scott Foster and injuries to James Reimer and Petr Mrazek in the same game put David Ayres in the spotlight, several emergency backup goaltenders were one play away from entering an NHL game. Ayres himself was in that spot three times before his 2020 appearance with the Carolina Hurricanes in Toronto, once each with the Maple Leafs, Red Wings, and Blackhawks.

On dozens of occasions, the emergency backup goalie has gotten dressed quietly without anyone outside the arena even finding out his name. A few times, the EBUG made it all the way to the bench in uniform and thought he was about to go in. The closest of close calls still belongs to Chris Levesque.

––––––––––––

Vancouver Canucks general manager Brian Burke wanted to avoid any scenario that would involve Levesque going in net for his team against the Pittsburgh Penguins on December 9,

2003. Starter Dan Cloutier's groin injury at the team's morning skate meant Johan Hedberg would start against Pittsburgh with Levesque, a goaltender at the University of British Columbia, dressing as the backup. Everyone knew Hedberg's penchant for leaving his crease to play the puck. As longtime Canucks forward Trevor Linden said in a TSN special, "Johan Hedberg was a pretty active goaltender. He liked to get out to his crease."

Before the game, Burke sat Hedberg down with a message.

"Look we got this kid," Burke recalled on TSN telling Hedberg. "He's a college kid. I certainly don't want to see him play, so stay in the paint."

Hedberg couldn't help himself. Late in the first period, he skated out well beyond the top of the right faceoff circle attempting to win a race to the puck. Penguins winger Konstanin Koltsov crashed into him, knocking Hedberg's mask off in the collision. Hedberg lay on the ice with his head down and legs flailing, and the arena went from oohs, aahs, and gasps to quiet.

"It's half, 'Oh my god, this kid's got to play,' and half, 'I'm gonna kill this Swede when I get my hands on him,'" Burke said on TSN.

Canucks players turned their heads to look at Levesque, who was sitting on the bench. He didn't react because he didn't see the collision when it happened. Big winger Todd Bertuzzi was standing in his way.

"He's not a small man. He doesn't make a very good window," Levesque said. "I had no idea what happened. I didn't even know he was down."

It was not until Bertuzzi sat down that Levesque saw Hedberg down in pain on the ice and stared up at the video board to watch the replay. Amid the buzz of the crowd and trainers attending to Hedberg, Levesque chewed a piece of gum on the bench but didn't get up. No one from the Canucks told him to get ready, so he waited.

What's going to happen now? Levesque thought. "There was obviously zero expectation of anything like that happening."

Zero expectation in part because it had been nearly half a century since an emergency backup goaltender entered an NHL game. All of a sudden, it was a real possibility for a 23-year-old university student.

On the ice, Hedberg knew something was wrong with his right wrist. A trainer asked him if he could keep playing.

"I don't really have a choice, do I?" Hedberg said on TSN. "I knew I had to play through it. I didn't want to put that kid in that situation. That would have been extremely tough for him."

From his spot on the bench, Levesque figured Hedberg shook off the cobwebs and was fine.

"OK, nothing serious here," Levesque thought. "Sit back and enjoy the show."

Hedberg stayed in the game and finished the rest of the period. At the first intermission, Levesque could tell Hedberg was hurt worse than he was letting on because he had to help the goalie take his gear off. Hedberg got taped up from his fingertips all the way up his arm. He acknowledged later he played through a broken wrist.

Hedberg allowed two more goals on 11 shots in the second and third periods, and the Canucks beat the Penguins 4–3 on Markus Naslund's overtime winner.

After getting cut from more than a dozen teams growing up, going undrafted and playing in the Manitoba Junior Hockey League, Levesque said of course he would have liked to get the chance of a lifetime to play in the NHL. He played the *What if?* game in his head for quite a few years before realizing it was not meant to be and would not have changed the trajectory of his life.

He now runs Levesque Goaltending Instruction in Grand Prairie, Alberta.

"It wasn't in the cards for me to play," he said on TSN. "It's just a cool Vancouver Canucks folklore story that just keeps living."

Rob Laurie was part of the first professional sporting event at the brand-new Arrowhead Pond in Anaheim, California, on July 2, 1993. He was the starting goaltender for the Anaheim Bullfrogs in a Roller Hockey International game.

Little did he know that 20 years later he'd be dressing for the NHL's Anaheim Ducks at age 42.

Laurie took a liking to goaltending as a kid growing up and playing in East Lansing, Michigan, first splitting the duties before taking over the net himself. He played 49 games of Division I college hockey over four seasons at Western Michigan from 1988 to '92.

Laurie turned that experience into a more than respectable minor league career mostly in the East Coast Hockey League, bouncing around from the Roanoke Valley Rampage to the Dayton Bombers, Johnstown Chiefs, Greensboro Monarchs, Toledo Storm, Tallahassee Tiger Sharks, and Huntington Blizzard through 1997.

He got into one American Hockey League for the Adirondack Red Wings during the '95–96 season and finished his playing career with stints in the Western Professional Hockey League, United Hockey League, and Central Hockey League before hanging up the pads in 2002.

A decade later, Laurie got to know Ducks goaltender Jonas Hiller and skated with players during informal summer workouts.

One day, Hiller called him out of the blue to join the Ducks for practice, and his presence became a semi-regular occurrence.

"I was just happy to go to one practice," Laurie said.

Then his phone rang on April 5, 2013, and his Ducks experience went to another level. Hiller was too sick to dress that night against the Dallas Stars, and senior VP of hockey operations David McNab asked if Laurie could get to the rink and back up Viktor Fasth. Minor leaguer Igor Bobkov was on his way from Norfolk, Virginia, but McNab didn't want to chance it.

Laurie was working as manager of goaltending outfitter Goalie Monkey and stopped in his tracks. He asked a coworker if he was going to the game tonight.

"I don't know, are you?" the coworker asked.

"Dude, I'm dressing," Laurie responded.

First, he had to dry out his equipment after a beer league game the previous night. Laurie sprawled everything out across his driveway so it could soak up some Southern California sunshine during the afternoon before it was time to go to the arena.

Laurie felt like a member of the team while sitting in the locker room beforehand. He was part of future Hockey Hall of Famer Teemu Selanne's pregame ritual of going around the room and saying something about every player in uniform.

"Let's hear it for Robby, first NHL game!" Selanne said, as though Laurie were a hot shot prospect called up from the minors.

Laurie saw Bobkov walk in after pregame warm-ups, take off his chest protector, and say to Ducks defenseman Luca Sbisa, "Well, my work's done here." He waited for the rest of the players to leave the room to take his gear off when veteran winger Corey Perry stopped at his stall.

"What are you doing? Perry asked.

"The other dude's here," Laurie said. "I'm done."

"You might as well go out there," Perry said. "He's not out here yet. Come on. Get your shit on."

Laurie realized that wasn't such a bad idea after all. He put the chest protector and his No. 43 Ducks jersey back on and took his place on the bench for the national anthem and start of the game.

He was there for almost the first four minutes of the first period when Bobkov tapped Laurie on the shoulder to tell him his work was actually done for the night.

But it was far from Laurie's last job as an emergency backup goaltender or his closest call.

Anaheim knew recently retired NHL-goalie-turned-goaltending-consultant Dwayne Roloson could dress in a pinch—and he did in November 2014. But at the start of the 2013–14 season, McNab asked Laurie to come to games and sit in the stands when Roloson wasn't there in case the Ducks needed someone in a hurry.

McNab was ahead of his time in making sure an extra goalie was in the arena, doing so four years before the NHL made it a requirement. Laurie, now 43, was in the midst of a four-game run of being Anaheim's emergency backup when he got a call on January 5, 2014, that the Vancouver Canucks might need someone because Roberto Luongo was injured.

False alarm. The Canucks had already found someone.

Oh, well, Laurie thought to himself. *I got to do it once already, and now someone else will get to do it.*

Laurie's sister was in town, and they sat down for a late lunch at Lucille's Smokehouse BBQ. He had already eaten a sizable brisket meal when the Canucks called to say their other goalie was ineligible and needed him after all—and the game was a 5 PM start.

He had to call McNab to let him know he couldn't serve as the Ducks emergency goalie that night because he was actually dressing as Vancouver's backup. Laurie was on the bench in a

No. 35 Canucks jersey when starter Eddie Lack was bowled over into the net and lay sprawled out on the ice.

Trainers attended to Lack, and Laurie thought, *Holy shit, I'm going in this game right now. This is too crazy.*

Lack got up, shook it off, and played the rest of the game on his 26th birthday.

"I would've wanted to go in, but I didn't want him to get hurt," Laurie said years later.

Less than three months later, Laurie got a call from old friend and then Chicago assistant coach Jamie Kompon while trying to get a sandwich at Jersey Mike's Subs. Someone from the Minnesota Wild had reached out to Kompon, who spent six years as a Los Angeles Kings assistant, to see if he knew a goalie in the area who could dress because of an injury to Darcy Kuemper.

This is getting out of hand, Laurie thought.

Fellow former minor league goalie Jim Mill, Minnesota's special assistant to general manager Chuck Fletcher, called Laurie to request his services to back up Ilya Bryzgalov. After several years being a Kings season ticket holder, Laurie was on the visiting bench wearing a No. 33 Wild jersey.

Bryzgalov made 18 saves, and Minnesota won to snap L.A.'s six-game winning streak. After a joyous celebration of a big win for the Wild, Laurie thought he was alone in the shower and wiped the soap out of his eyes when he heard a voice say, "So, are you coming to Chicago with us?" It was Bryzgalov.

"You and me, we make a good goalie tandem," Bryzgalov said.

The Wild went on to Chicago without Laurie and made it to the second round of the playoffs before losing to the Blackhawks. The Kings went on to win the Stanley Cup a few months later, their second NHL championship in three years.

Laurie remains the only emergency backup goaltender to dress for three different NHL teams in two different buildings.

Santino Vasquez was watching the New York Rangers–Minnesota Wild game on his couch the night of December 17, 2015. He had just gotten home from his coaching job and put his equipment on the radiator to dry out when he saw Wild defenseman Marco Scandella's shot strike Rangers starting goaltender Antti Raanta in the mask not even 14 minutes into the game.

Raanta went down, and Henrik Lundqvist entered in relief. Vasquez had agreed to be the backup goalie available to either team in case of emergency, and until that point it had mostly been a joke among friends other than his father telling him you never know when the call is going to come.

Then it happened. Wild strength and conditioning coach Kirk Olson called and asked Vasquez if he could get to the arena with his gear.

Vasquez packed up and made the two-mile drive from his place in St. Paul to Xcel Energy Center.

"I played it cool, but I was almost in a panic," Vasquez wrote on The Players Tribune a few days later. His experience to that point included semi-pro hockey in the Czech Republic and two games of Division III college hockey at Hamline University over the previous two years.

Vasquez arrived early in the second period and was escorted to an auxiliary locker room. He was soon told to get dressed just in case and started stretching out.

He had skated with Rangers center Derek Stepan before. But that didn't stop Stepan from seeing Vasquez, doing a double take, and asking incredulously, "You're the emergency goalie?" They shared some small talk, and Vasquez stayed ready.

"I don't really get too nervous," he told the *St. Paul Pioneer Press* at the time. "I've been down here a lot. I would have been ready to play, that's for sure. I know they wouldn't have scored on me every shot."

Vasquez never got to find out. Lundqvist played the final 46-plus minutes of New York's 5–2 loss, and Vasquez packed up his gear and went home.

"It's part of the game," Rangers coach Alain Vigneault lamented that night. So was Vasquez's job to be ready when called upon as an emergency backup.

———————

Eric Semborski was already a cult hero for the Chicago Blackhawks from the game he dressed for them in Philadelphia in 2016. Later that same season, he got even closer to entering an NHL game—and for the Flyers he grew up rooting for.

How close? Semborski was in the crease.

The day of April 1, 2017, developed much slower for Semborski than 17 months earlier when he frantically rushed home from one rink to get his gear and showed up at Wells Fargo Center to back up for Chicago after Corey Crawford had an emergency appendectomy. The chaos was happening within the Flyers organization.

Steve Mason was supposed to start at home against the New Jersey Devils, but he was sick and ruled out in the morning. Michal Neuvirth moved into the starting role, and the Flyers sought to recall Anthony Stolarz from the minors. Stolarz was with the American Hockey League's Lehigh Valley Phantoms, who were on their way from Allentown to Wilkes-Barre Township, Pennsylvania, to face the Penguins' top affiliate.

Stolarz was scheduled to dress for the Phantoms that night, but when the bus arrived in Wilkes-Barre, he had a car service from the Flyers waiting and needed to get to Philadelphia to back up Neuvirth. Stolarz should get there on time, but the Flyers told Semborski to come to the arena with his gear just in case. Stolarz beat puck drop by a few minutes, walking in just as players were going on the ice.

Semborski stood down, took the elevator up to the press box, and started watching the game. Stolarz hurriedly got dressed and was stationed on the bench a few minutes into the first period.

After a stoppage in play 7:37 in, Neuvirth was alone in his crease awaiting a faceoff at the far end of the ice when he fell backward toward the net. Flyers trainer Jim McCrossin ran to attend to the 29-year-old and was joined by three team doctors. Neuvirth appeared to be unconscious for a short period of time but began moving his arms and legs and sat up in the crease before being placed on a stretcher and carted off.

"It's obviously pretty scary when you see your goaltender just collapse like that," Flyers forward Chris VandeVelde said that night. "I'm not sure really what happened, if he fainted or got lightheaded or what, but it was pretty scary and I'm glad to see he was moving and functioning when he was rolled off the ice."

Watching from high above the ice, Semborski saw Neuvirth collapse and did not have much time to react. Within seconds, team officials grabbed him to escort him down to the locker room to get ready. At ice level, Stolarz went into the game ice cold with the Flyers leading 1–0.

"I didn't really have much time to warm up or anything like that," Stolarz said. "It was kind of a hectic day altogether."

In just the fifth NHL appearance of his rookie season, the native of Edison, New Jersey, stopped all 26 shots the Devils put on net and Philadelphia built up a 3–0 lead. Semborski put his gear on and watched from a television monitor in the tunnel connecting the locker room to the bench. Philadelphia's players knew Semborski and wanted him to get in the game. When he dressed for Chicago, he was one Flyers empty-net goal from going in the net against them in garbage time.

After Stolarz made his 26th save of the night with 24.5 seconds left, coach Dave Hakstol motioned to the end of the bench and Semborski was told, "Sembo, let's go." Semborski put on his mask and was handed his stick, and he skated to the crease to relieve Stolarz.

"Guys on the bench wanted him in," Hakstol said. "Guys are pulling for a young man in that situation. It was a point of the game where we could do it."

Wearing an orange No. 49 jersey with no nameplate that might've once belonged to Michael Leighton, Semborski stretched in the crease, tapped each goal post, and got ready for the faceoff. Before they could drop the puck, referees Eric Furlatt and Justin St-Pierre interrupted. Because Semborski was an emergency backup, he could only enter the game if Stolarz was injured.

"As soon as they blew the whistle and the ref was skating over to the bench, I knew that this isn't going to fly," Semborski said.

Boos—for the officials, not Semborski—rained down from the crowd and he gave fans a wave as he exited the game almost as quickly as he entered. Stolarz resumed his spot in the crease. Hakstol certainly didn't regret giving it a try.

"Unfortunately it didn't work out where he actually got to play a few seconds," he said. "He at least did get out there and got in the crease for a couple of seconds."

Semborski called it a class-act move by Hakstol to try to put him in the game.

"Not too much could've went wrong," he said. "But with a shutout on the line, just to have a little confidence in me and the respect to try to give this kid some time is pretty cool."

Standing in the crease for the few seconds he was allowed to be there, Semborski could see Devils players staring at him like they were going to fire at will. Regardless of the outcome, it was a moment he'll never forget. "It was really cool to get out there and get set for a faceoff," he said.

Stolarz was filled with immediate regret. In the locker room afterward, he told Semborski, "Man, if I would've known, I would have faked something."

A few years later, Stolarz said he absolutely would have faked a minor injury and that the referees that night "kind of ruined the fun."

"For him to have that opportunity to go in there for that amount of time, that would have been great," Stolarz said. "It would've been a dream come true for him. I'm sure he relished the moment just being able to step on that ice in front of that crowd and kind of just hear the cheers."

———————

Friday the 13th turned out to be a lucky day for Ben Hause in December 2019. He was tired from a long week of work at his day job at Dish Network and had done two other emergency backup goaltender games for the Avalanche in the previous four days—and he was scheduled to do it again when they hosted the Devils. Watching the second period, he noticed New Jersey starter Louis Domingue doing some extra stretching—more than usual for a healthy goalie.

"That kind of was my first red flag that he was clearly not doing well," Hause said.

At the next TV timeout, Domingue went to the bench to talk to a team trainer, who asked if he was OK to continue playing. Domingue shook his head no and went down the tunnel, and Mackenzie Blackwood entered the game.

This is it, Hause thought. *Now we're up.*

He started texting friends and family to let them know he was getting in uniform. Within minutes, Hause's Avalanche contact found him and ushered him to the Devils locker room. Of all the times Hause was the EBUG, of course he got this opportunity with New Jersey.

Born in 1989 and growing up in Minnesota, Hause was in what he calls "hockey limbo" since the North Stars left for Dallas in 1993 and the Wild didn't come into existence until 2000. Because he was a goalie, he began idolizing future Hall of Famer Martin Brodeur and his room was full of Devils paraphernalia. His grandparents took a photo of him in a white Devils jersey at age six after getting it as a Christmas present.

Hause walked into organized chaos in the visiting locker room in Denver. Trainers were evaluating Domingue's injury, assistant GM Tom Fitzgerald was trying to get Hause's paperwork in order while figuring out how to get another goalie to Phoenix the next day, and equipment staffers were beginning the process of packing up for the team's postgame departure. When it was clear Domingue would not return, Hause signed his amateur tryout contract and started to get dressed. He was handed a white Devils jersey with the No. 65 and no name on it.

"That's when it started to feel, like, really real and really like, 'Oh, shit. One more injury and I'm going to be on the ice in an NHL game,'" Hause said. Thoughts raced through his head about Blackwood going into a game cold at altitude and how he'd never played in a game of this magnitude.

Hause was shuffled into the trainers' room at the second intermission so he would be out of sight, out of mind for Devils players in the middle of their game. He watched the third period with Connor Carrick and the rest of the team's scratches and support staff. Hause didn't get to keep the jersey, but he did get a picture taken of himself wearing it that his parents framed with the one of him as a child on Santa's lap. He also kept the contract as a souvenir of the closest he got to the NHL.

Taxi squads during the shortened 2021 season that required a third goaltender around at all times should have prevented even the possibility of a scare. But a bizarre sequence of events on April 24 in Vancouver left the Ottawa Senators one injury away from putting forward Artem Anisimov in net.

Anton Forsberg was projected to start, just like he was in line for Chicago on March 29, 2018, when Scott Foster got in. Forsberg was again injured during pregame workouts.

"He's a magnet," Foster said. "I'm going to make sure I don't take any games that he's around."

Matt Murray moved into the starting role with taxi squad goalie Marcus Hogberg backing up against the Canucks. Murray had recently missed more than a month with an undisclosed injury but had won three in a row since returning. After a collision just over four minutes into the second period on a play he was penalized for tripping, Murray exited the game with a brand-new injury.

When Hogberg entered, Anisimov was instructed to leave his perch in the press box to go down to the locker room and put on the goalie gear. Hogberg finished the game without issue, but as Anisimov said on his Instagram account, he was more than ready to make his NHL goaltending debut

"We had Arty dressed and ready to go," coach D.J. Smith told reporters that night. "We didn't have anyone left. It's a tough situation, but Arty had the gear on and was ready to go in."

Center Colin White wondered if Anisimov would have performed just as well as Ayres 14 months earlier. Injured Senators goaltender Joey D'Accord tweeted, "Arty's been playing the wrong position all along."

Anisimov would have been the first skater to play goal in an NHL game since Jerry Toppazzini in 1960. Even though he didn't get in, he gave his teammates some entertainment.

"Definitely loosens up things a little bit after the game in the locker room to see him dressed up as a goalie," Ottawa defenseman Thomas Chabot said. "It's weird stuff happening, guys get hurt, and obviously to see him dressed up, it was pretty funny. The guys definitely had a good little laugh at it, but I mean it's good on him, good for Arty being ready to play goalie in case we needed him."

It also gave Foster a laugh when buddies sent him pictures of Anisimov in goalie gear, especially knowing that was him three years earlier when Forsberg was injured.

CHAPTER 12

GEARING UP: WHAT GOES INTO SERVING AS AN EMERGENCY BACKUP

GOALTENDERS TEND TO BE CREATURES OF HABIT, especially on a game day. There's a specific routine with some superstitions and exercises to get the mind and body right to play the most important position in hockey.

Emergency backup goaltenders? That's a mixed bag.

In the hours leading up to Scott Foster's one-time NHL appearance for the Chicago Blackhawks, he took his daughters to school, rode the train into the city to work his day job as an accountant, and reversed the trip home before going to the rink. David Ayres enjoyed a morning with his family and went to the gym with his wife for a session of heavy leg workouts.

"Everybody approaches it differently," Foster said. "I'm sure there's some guys that treat it almost like game day, and maybe that's what I should have been thinking differently. I have a job, I've got to do it, but I know my schedule. I know that I'm going to be there when I need to be there. I'm going to be prepared. But the rest of my day is not taken up preparing to be an emergency goalie."

Justin Goldman was one of those guys who needed to treat EBUG assignments like games, to the point that he needed to make sure he could get off from his day job because he couldn't focus. He was anxious for hours on end thinking about the slim chance of getting in.

"You're like, 'OK, 99.9 percent sure nothing's going to happen, so I'm not going to stress out. I'm not going to worry. I'm not going to prepare as if this is the biggest game of my life,'" Goldman said. "But holy shit, there's that 0.1 percent chance this could be the biggest day of my life."

Goldman and his fellow Colorado Avalanche EBUGs had a specific routine when they got to the arena: drop your gear off outside the locker room a couple of hours before the game and take your seat to watch the game. And, naturally, stay ready.

But what does it mean to be ready? Playing some kind of men's league hockey and perhaps not having a double cheeseburger with fries and soda for lunch on a game day.

"All of us have day jobs. Most of us have families. We don't have the luxury of getting six or seven days' worth of practice," said Denver-based emergency backup goaltender Ben Hause, who was one injury away from playing for the New Jersey Devils against the Avalanche in December 2019. "We don't have the luxury of having a gym and access to trainers and nutritionists and this, that and the other. So, you really do have to make an extremely conscious effort on those game days when you're up."

Even though Ayres was 42 when he went in for the Carolina Hurricanes on February 22, 2020, the kidney transplant recipient stayed in shape by avoiding beer and working out regularly. If anything, he might have pushed himself harder than he should have if he had known he was playing in the NHL that night.

"I knew that was my day. I knew I had to go to the rink that night," Ayres said. "I was just going there to basically watch hockey, and if I was called upon, then sure."

Of course, Ayres was called upon and stopped eight of the 10 shots he faced. Only after the adrenaline wore off late in the game did he start to feel the effects.

"Good thing we had a decent lead there because all of a sudden from that heavy workout you're starting to feel heavy and a little bit shaky," Ayres said.

In recent years, the NHL has put specific qualifications into who can serve as an EBUG. When Tom Fenton got the call to dress for the Phoenix Coyotes in 2010, he hadn't played in an organized hockey game in 18 months. Nathan Schoenfeld hadn't played competitively in 10 years when the Coyotes needed him in a pinch in 2016.

NHL rules that were updated in 2017 required emergency backup goaltender candidates to play some sort of men's league hockey. They can't be professionals, but they need to be on the ice regularly, which helps teams know what kind of standard they're getting across the league.

Hause plays in a competitive men's league in Denver, but that's once a week, so he puts in a concerted effort to skate and be sharp when he has an EBUG game coming up. He tries to line up drop-in skates and other pick-up games to practice so he's not rusty.

"Just to get some more shots and just to get some more familiarity," he said. "But that's all on your own. That's all self-motivated, self-driven. It's up to you to go out and secure the ice or get a men's league game to play in or whatever it is."

Montreal EBUG Sean Kelly, a chemical engineer, skated with NHL players and other professionals and felt like it always gave him a puncher's chance.

"I'm not at the level that I used to play," Kelly said when he was 28 in early 2021. "But I know if all the stars are aligned, I can do a decent job. I think I can do the job if called upon."

Kelly's closest call came when the Canadiens were hosting the Toronto Maple Leafs and Frederik Andersen stayed down on the ice for a few seconds after a collision. Kelly was sitting next to Montreal prospect Cayden Primeau in the Bell Centre press box.

Primeau looked at Kelly and said, "This might be your chance." While the nerves kicked in for Kelly at that point, Andersen stayed in the game and he stood down.

Kelly approached EBUG days like he did game days when he was playing competitively—and that means trying not to think too much about the playing.

"In my own experience, if I do get tense during the day, I will suck if I get on the ice," he said. "So I just try to stay loose and if it has to happen, it'll happen. There's no use worrying about it beforehand. Now, that's easy to say, but applying it isn't always easy."

It was plenty easy for Foster, whose routine upon arriving at United Center in Chicago involved eating dinner at the second intermission in the press box, enjoying a cup of Peanut M&Ms, and going home. After stopping all seven shots he faced in his one and only NHL game in 2018, though, he worried about what his mindset would be like going back to work as an EBUG.

"Now I'd be showing up to games thinking, 'Oh crap, am I going to play?' all day," Foster said. "It's almost like an innocence that's gone."

Foster took a game the following season, and he agreed after some initial hesitation.

"It's like, 'Hey, we need help. Bring your family, sit in a box, watch the game,'" he said. "They're all having a great time and I'm chewing on my nails."

Foster returned to the job full time, at first asking the Blackhawks if they needed help filling games and eventually getting back in their rotation.

"You realize that it is cool," he said. "It's neat to do and it's fun and it's a connection to hockey. For a period of my life, so much of it was a huge component of my life and I get a bunch of that with the guys that I play with, but it's not the same. You get a taste of that seriousness, and you want to get back to that game."

Foster started sitting in a folding chair on the 200 level and began getting recognized. He was often asked if he worked for one of the teams because he would not react to anything going on during the game.

"Apparently I just have no reaction to anything I'm seeing on the ice," Foster said. "I'm emotionless."

It's far different than when Foster goes to a game with his daughters and allows himself to be a bit of a fan. But he has felt more at home in the press box.

"I'm just watching hockey, and that's it," he said. "It was just a great way to watch a game and kind of be a hockey geek about it."

On days that Kelly would serve as EBUG in Montreal, the bulk of his anxiety came while at work waiting to leave at 3 PM. Anything after that was icing on the cake.

"To me it's fun, and it gets me energized for the day," Kelly said. "I don't have trouble concentrating at all. To me, it's really exciting because I get to go watch an NHL hockey game for free."

CHAPTER 13

UNRETIRED FOR A NIGHT: EX-NHL GOALTENDERS JUMP BACK IN

Fred Brathwaite could see the players on the other team staring over at him from across the ice wondering what was going on. Brathwaite had played in 255 NHL games but not in almost two decades. He also stood 5'7" and was 48 years old.

"They're looking at you and they're kind of giggling like, 'What's this fat guy doing?'" Brathwaite said. "I probably looked like their dad. They were licking their chops hoping our goalie was going to get hurt, that's for sure."

Brathwaite dressed as the backup goaltender under emergency conditions for the Henderson Silver Knights of the American Hockey League for their game at the San Diego Gulls on April 24, 2021.

Imagine doing that in the NHL? A few of Brathwaite's contemporaries have had to do exactly that when there wasn't another goalie available long after their playing days were over.

Robb Tallas played 99 games in the NHL from 1996 to 2001, mostly with the Boston Bruins and a dozen at the end with the Chicago Blackhawks. He spent two more years in the American Hockey League, was one of the best goalies in Finland in 2003–04, and played one more season in Austria before hanging up his pads for good.

Or so he thought.

Tallas was into his fourth season as goaltending coach of the Florida Panthers in 2013 when his background came in handy. Starter Jose Theodore was injured minutes into their game at Carolina on Saturday, March 2, and they played at home against the Panthers the next night. Scott Clemmensen was set for back-to-back duty in net and the team called up prospect Jacob Markstrom.

Markstrom made it. His goalie gear did not.

Nothing else would fit the 6'6" Swede, so the Panthers needed a backup plan. They turned to a former backup in Tallas, who at 39 signed a professional tryout agreement worth $500.

As relaxed as Clemmensen usually was in his preparation, Tallas told him not to let his presence in uniform be any kind of a distraction. Tallas so badly didn't want to mess with Clemmensen's head or anyone else's that he got dressed in his office and returned there after pregame warm-ups.

"They still had a game to play," he said.

Tallas took his place in full uniform at the end of the bench but didn't worry much about the prospect of going into the game. If he had? Tallas figured coaching gave him some extra knowledge to add to his playing repertoire, even if he rarely wore goalie skates and put the gear on anymore.

"You'd go out and I'd obviously try to do my best and everything," he said. "You would hope that some of the stuff you had done your whole life would come back. I think obviously being a coach, you had a much greater mind for the game, and you could actually think a lot more and predict things and hopefully that would have helped the situation."

Playing at 39 was nothing for Dwayne Roloson. He was an NHL goaltender for four more seasons after his 39th birthday and backstopped the Tampa Bay Lightning to the 2011 Eastern Conference final at 42. He made one All-Star Game but was best known for carrying the Edmonton Oilers to the 2006 Stanley Cup Final before an injury in the series opener cut short his chances of winning the Conn Smythe Trophy as playoff MVP.

Roloson's career spanned hockey eras as he played 656 NHL games from 1996 to 2012 with the Calgary Flames, Buffalo Sabres, Minnesota Wild, Oilers, New York Islanders, and Lightning. He went right into coaching as a volunteer assistant at his alma mater, the University of Massachusetts Lowell, in 2012–13 and became a goaltending consultant for the Norfolk Admirals of the American Hockey League. The next season, he was goaltending consultant for the Anaheim Ducks, the team he beat in the 2006 West final.

At least when the Ducks needed him on November 2, 2014, at age 45, he was less than three years removed from playing in the NHL.

The team knew Frederik Andersen would not be able to play at the Colorado Avalanche because of leg tightness and recalled journeyman Jason LaBarbera from Norfolk to back up rookie John Gibson. Roloson took part in the morning skate that day opposite Gibson while LaBarbera, on two hours of sleep, took two long flights to make it to Denver shortly before the game.

Gibson was in line to start, until he stepped on a puck during pregame warm-up and it was clear he would not be available. Roloson was already up in the press box getting his notes together when his phone started going off. He was surprised Ducks staffers were calling from down by the ice because he figured they were preparing for their own pregame meetings. He finally picked up and was told, "Hey, you got to get down here. You got to get dressed."

One plus? Roloson was accustomed to putting on the pads and mask and practicing with the Ducks that season. He geared up, put on a white No. 79 jersey, and took his place at the end of the bench while LaBarbera made his first NHL start since the previous December.

LaBarbera, who played a full game each of the previous two days for Norfolk, allowed two goals on 11 shots in the first period. Coach Bruce Boudreau looked down the bench at Roloson and said, "Make sure you're ready."

"I got a little nervous," Roloson said. "I started getting a little antsy about that."

If he had gotten into the game, Roloson would have been the third-oldest goaltender to play in the NHL. He was ready.

"I practiced a fair amount, so it wasn't like it was going to be like coming in cold turkey," he said. "Plus, mentally, going through a career and understanding ups and downs and getting thrown in after a guy gets pulled and going through those situations before, I think it makes it a lot easier."

It was even easier because Anaheim came back to win and give LaBarbera his first NHL victory in 13 months.

"He played well," Roloson. "We ended up winning that night, which was a good bonus."

———————

It was just over two weeks after Roloson's game when another retired goalie was forced into uniform. Only Arturs Irbe was far less prepared to come out of retirement for a night. He just didn't have much of a choice.

Growing up in Latvia when it was still part of the Soviet Union, Irbe played his first few professional seasons with Dynamo Riga in the Russian Superleague before moving to North America in 1991 to join the expansion San Jose Sharks.

He played 619 games over 13 NHL seasons for the Sharks, Dallas Stars, Vancouver Canucks, and Carolina Hurricanes and finished in the top 10 of voting for the Vezina Trophy as the league's top goalie three times. He helped Carolina reach the Stanley Cup Final in 2002, played his final NHL game in 2004, and finished his playing career in Europe.

Irbe wasn't at all prepared to *be* a goalie again on November 18, 2014, which just happened to be Independence Day in Latvia. He was 47 and in his first season as goaltending coach of the Buffalo Sabres. There was also one of those Western New York snowstorms going on outside.

During the first period against the Sharks, Buffalo starter Michal Neuvirth fell awkwardly back into the net and left with an injury. Jhonas Enroth entered the game as Neuvirth's replacement. "We started scrambling, looking for options," Irbe told reporters that night. "And it's a snow day."

Coach Ted Nolan called on Irbe to gear up as the backup, asking, "Arch, why don't you be our security net, just in case?"

"Ted, I haven't donned a uniform in seven years,'" Irbe said.

"It doesn't matter," Nolan replied. "Now you will."

Much like Brathwaite, Irbe at 5'8" didn't fit the height requirement for a modern-day goaltender. Fortunately for him, Enroth was close at 5'10", so Irbe donned an extra pair of Enroth's pads. He grabbed an old glove and blocker left behind by former Sabres netminder Ryan Miller and pieced the outfit together with a mask unearthed by the equipment staff.

"It's not the comfortable equipment I'm used to," Irbe said after the game. "But I had to persevere, put it on. It took a while. Much longer than it usually takes—it's been seven years. And that was it."

Irbe signed his one-day, professional tryout contract and was dressed and ready during the second intermission. He stood in the tunnel early in the third period psyching himself up about the possibility of playing in an NHL game for the first time in a decade.

"It was the atmosphere, that feeling that you're back there by the bench and the game is going on and you're pulling for your team," Irbe said then. "I was thinking how I would approach it if I had to go in, visualizing—the best part of the game."

Much to the disappointment of countryman Zemgus Girgensons, Irbe didn't get a chance to step into the net in the third period. He did have fun imagining the possibility.

"Be careful what you wish for," Irbe said with a smile. "Obviously, I didn't want Jhonny to get hurt or something bad happen. But if I would go in, I would have had fun. I know that.

"Once a goalie, always a goalie."

———————————

Once an EBUG, always an EBUG for Tallas, who got his second scare the night of the Panthers goaltending fiasco in March 2015. The closest he got to the ice was the end of the tunnel in full uniform before Roberto Luongo was back from the hospital and relieved injured teammate Al Montoya in net.

As rare and strange a scenario as that was, Florida general manager Dale Tallon pointed out, "It happened one more time that year."

Before the end of the month, the Boston Bruins were in a jam when starter Tuukka Rask had to leave the game 10 seconds into the second period because of severe dehydration. Niklas Svedberg took over, and the Bruins had a blueprint from the Panthers to follow to make sure another backup was ready.

Goaltending coach Bob Essensa suited up at age 50. Had anything happened to Svedberg, Essensa would have shattered Maurice 'Moe' Roberts' record as the oldest goalie to appear in the NHL. Essensa last played in the NHL in 2002 with the Sabres.

———————

Brathwaite figures that if he had gotten into Henderson's game in 2021, he would have played behind the best defense of his life.

"We would have had guys who never block shots probably blocking shots for me," he said. "You never really know what would have happened or could have happened. But I'm betting most of my players would've been blocking shots and trying to do whatever they could so the puck wouldn't get to me."

Brathwaite joked he would have only allowed five goals, which was about the norm in his playing days.

Of course, he only got the chance to dress by that time because he was coaching in the AHL. When the NHL formalized new emergency backup goaltending procedures a few years earlier, the league eliminated the possibility of retired professionals doing the job. At first, it was a salary cap problem because pros had to get paid at least $500. Then, the rules specified that the available EBUGs were not allowed to have played professional hockey.

As comfortable as Roloson felt stepping in as the backup, he's happy with the way a standard has been set across the league.

"If you leave it to the teams, then you just never know what you're going to get," he said. "I honestly think that the league has done a great job with making sure that they have somebody in the building. It's more than they had before any of this. It's great that the league has taken it into their hands. You've got to make sure it's [someone] that's definitely serviceable or has actually played the position just in case the situation arises that the guy has to go in."

CHAPTER 14

AFTER INTERMISSION: EMERGENCY BACKUPS RETURN AFTER SHUTDOWN

THE COVID-19 PANDEMIC that began weeks after David Ayres' magical performance for the Carolina Hurricanes brought the 2019–20 NHL season to a halt on March 12. While hockey resumed with the playoffs in quarantine bubbles in Canada, the emergency backup goaltender program was on ice for more than 18 months.

All 24 teams that were part of the expanded postseason in the summer and fall brought at least three goaltenders into the bubble. When the NHL came back for a condensed, 56-game 2021 season in 31 home arenas, each team carried a taxi squad of players and was required to have a third goalie around at all times. Because of coronavirus protocols, EBUGs were put on pause.

"You don't realize how much you miss it and appreciate it until it's gone, until we had the shutdown," Colorado Avalanche emergency backup goaltender Ben Hause said. "The more you get to reflect on it and think back, the more I think I even appreciated how special and how amazing that role is."

When the NHL announced the 2021–22 season would begin in October and go for 82 games, teams began preparing for a return to normalcy after 18 months of pandemic-interrupted hockey. Taxi squads were still an open question when training camps opened in September, with the league wanting to see how things went. Ultimately, they were abandoned in favor of traditional 23-man rosters for a majority of the season.

That meant assistant general managers and front office staff reconnecting with local goaltenders to get every home game covered. Within the first three-plus months of the season, four emergency backup goaltenders got to experience varying degrees of life in the NHL.

Alex Bishop

Alex Bishop likes to tell people that he didn't choose to be a goaltender as much as the position chose him. Growing up in the early 2000s in Richmond Hill, Ontario, outside Toronto, no one on his first youth team wanted to go in net, so Bishop volunteered. He wasn't even supposed to play in what turned out to be his first season of recreational hockey, until the coach called his father to say the team needed a goalie.

He played goal throughout childhood, including two years in the Greater Toronto Hockey League, which has produced countless NHL goalies, including 2019 Stanley Cup winner Jordan Binnington, Kevin Weekes, Sean Burke, and Bob Essensa.

From there? "It definitely wasn't a straight path," Bishop said.

He began playing for Newmarket and Hamilton in the Ontario Junior Hockey League—a step below the major junior level—at age 16. The next year, in 2014, he advanced to the Quebec Major Junior Hockey League with the Saint John Sea Dogs. Bishop bounced around the QMJHL to the Quebec

Remparts and Val d'Or Foreurs, playing 76 games in the league until he turned 20.

Bishop's hockey journey brought him back to the Toronto area with the OJHL's Markham Royals before he asked for a trade and ended up out in Prince Edward Island playing for the Summerside Western Capitals of the Maritime Hockey League. It was there that he decided to commit to the University of Toronto.

When the NHL adjusted its emergency backup goaltending rules in 2017 to require each team to have a list of possibilities available and an EBUG at the ready for each home game, the Maple Leafs began a program that included a rotation of university players from around the area, along with seasoned practice goalie David Ayres. Bishop arrived at the University of Toronto in 2018 and immediately began filling that role on game nights.

"It's more just having my gear at the rink, being ready," Bishop said. "I'm definitely not in the stands drinking beers and eating hot dogs."

When Ayres got the call to go into the game for the Hurricanes, it was close to being Bishop's turn. Bishop was the emergency backup for the Maple Leafs' next game after Ayres, so the odds were not in his favor.

"Two in a row would be something else," he said.

The NHL put that season on pause less than three weeks later, and emergency backup goalies were not needed during the shortened 2021 season. It took only five days into the following season for one to be needed.

Petr Mrazek, coincidentally the same goaltender whose injury opened the door for Ayres, was injured in his Maple Leafs debut on Thursday night, October 14, midway through their game at the Ottawa Senators. The team was right up against the salary cap, so general manager Kyle Dubas and assistant GM Brandon Pridham had to come up with a creative solution.

University of Toronto coach Ryan Medel called Bishop on Friday night to tell him about an interesting opportunity. Bishop found out he was at least joining the Maple Leafs for their morning skate Saturday and may be needed to back up, pending the results of Mrazek's MRI.

When Bishop got to the game arena, he found out he'd be going on the ice with 2021 leading goal-scorer Auston Matthews, who was working his way back from wrist surgery. He got the pep talk not to let Matthews destroy his confidence before going on the ice with the reigning Rocket Richard Trophy winner.

"He has a good shot," Bishop deadpanned hours later. "He's a pretty good player. I just did my best. I had a good time."

After 40 minutes of taking shots from Matthews, Bishop stayed on the ice for Toronto's full team morning skate and held his own.

"I didn't score any on him, so he looked pretty good," forward Alexander Kerfoot said.

By the time Bishop got back to the locker room, his phone had blown up with text messages. Word had gotten out in the press that the Maple Leafs would be signing him to an amateur tryout contract for the day to back up starter Jack Campbell.

"Most of my friends and teammates knew that I was backing up that night before I did," he said. He was getting so many messages he eventually turned the phone off entirely.

Bishop got a bite to eat at the arena before heading home. His typical game day routine involves a nap, but he knew there was no chance of getting any rest on the verge of his first game in an NHL uniform. With his university team on the road for an exhibition game in nearby Guelph, his four housemates were gone, and the place was eerily quiet while all the thoughts of dressing for the Maple Leafs raced through his head.

What the peace and quiet did give Bishop was the chance to study. Between the morning skate that included taking shots from one of hockey's best goal-scorers and the chance of a lifetime to be one injury away from playing in the NHL, the commerce student specializing in finance and economics had to study for an upcoming midterm.

Bishop showered and returned to the rink to do his job for the night. With his parents in attendance, he joined the Maple Leafs for pregame warm-ups and sat on the bench for the game like any other backup goaltender.

"[Players] didn't really treat me any differently," he said after the game. "Everyone came and gave me daps and talked to me on the bench when they weren't really focused on the play."

Bishop spent the first period riding out the nerves that eased in the second and then spent the third soaking in the experience. His University of Toronto teammates missed warm-ups, but because their game at Guelph was in the afternoon, a handful made sure they were there for Bishop's big night.

"We bought tickets and once we got back from Guelph we went straight down to the rink and got to watch Bish," housemate and fellow goalie Jett Alexander said. "It was a pretty amazing moment, and we just wanted to be able to share it with him."

Bishop joked afterward that he kept trying to get the attention of former Saint John teammate Thomas Chabot, by then Ottawa's top defensemen and one of the best young players in the NHL, but Chabot never acknowledged him.

He never factored into the game, either, as Campbell stopped 20 of 21 shots to help the Maple Leafs beat the Senators 3–1. Less than 19 months since his team was beaten by Ayres the EBUG, coach Sheldon Keefe said he never once thought about the possibility of needing to turn to Bishop.

"Jack got through the game and was good and comfortable," he said afterward. "You go into the game thinking positively, so you're not too concerned about the backup goaltender. Lucky for us, we didn't need it."

Asked after the game what he'd take out of this chance, Bishop considered himself the lucky one.

"It's not lost on me that this is a pretty rare opportunity," he said. "Not a lot of people, if any, get to do things like this."

The next time it happened, it was closer to home than Bishop ever would have imagined.

Jett Alexander

Growing up on his parents' farm in Prince Edward County, Ontario, about a two-hour drive east of Toronto, Jett Alexander was always working with his hands. He credits that upbringing for pushing him toward the study of environmental science, and with that in childhood came a love of all things goaltending.

Like most kids who become goalies, he loved the masks and gear of those he was watching in the NHL in the mid to late 2000s. He tried it out at age six and never looked back.

"I've always loved the compete level you need to bring," Alexander said. "It's definitely a different mental game from forwards, and I think I've always just kind of found that challenge fun."

Goaltending took Alexander through the Greater Toronto Hockey League in his teenage years with the Don Mills Flyers and North York Rangers. He played for North York and the Georgetown Raiders in the Ontario Junior Hockey League before moving out west to British Columbia in 1999 just before his 20th birthday for an opportunity in arguably the best Tier 2 junior league in Canada. He played 40 games for the Prince George Spruce Kings of the British Columbia Hockey League before the combination of hockey and schooling led him to the University of Toronto.

"It was the right fit," he said. "It was a pretty easy decision."

Canadian university sports did not have a season in 2020–21 because of the pandemic, but Alexander bided his time and was ready to make his debut for the University of Toronto in the fall of 2021.

The morning of December 1 wasn't anything out of the ordinary. He went to class, worked out with teammates, and had practice. Alexander was scheduled to be the emergency backup goaltender that night for the Maple Leafs' game against the Colorado Avalanche, but the assignment changed when he stepped off the ice, checked his phone, and saw a missed call from Maple Leafs assistant GM Brandon Pridham. When Alexander called back, Pridham told him that one of Colorado's goalies was hurt and to get to the arena early just in case. He didn't know it was starter Darcy Kuemper—only that the Avalanche were frantically trying to get minor leaguer Justus Annunen to Toronto from their top affiliate based in Loveland, Colorado.

Fortunately for Alexander, his ride to the arena was also his EBUG for the night—Alex Bishop, his housemate who dressed for the Maple Leafs six and a half weeks earlier.

"We were kind of able to go through that together, so it was pretty special that way," Bishop said.

There were no guarantees, but Alexander took the required COVID-19 test, signed an amateur tryout contract, and was told he'd at least be skating in pregame warm-ups with the Avalanche. Because of protocols, Alexander couldn't dress in the locker room with the rest of Colorado's players and was the last one on the ice. On the bright side, with far less notice but no road trip to get in their way, Bishop, a handful of University of Toronto teammates and Alexander's girlfriend were able to be there on the glass for his 20 minutes of warm-up.

"It was crazy to soak it in," Alexander said. "It was pretty special just to look up and look at the jumbotron and see my friends and everyone on the glass banging on the glass as I skated by."

Then it turned into a waiting game. Alexander watched the first period by himself until Annunen arrived and took the backup's spot on the bench with Jonas Johansson starting. He was now two injuries away from being needed, so he took his gear off and joined his entourage in the stands for the rest of the game.

Alexander received an autographed stick from Colorado captain Gabriel Landeskog and has his Avalanche jersey hanging up in his room, but his fondest memory might be not letting anyone beat him clean on the 10 or so shots he faced in warm-ups. His roommates had video evidence of that perfect record.

"We were kind of joking once I got in the stands, 'Did you not let in a goal there?'" Alexander recalled. "I was like, 'No, I didn't.' That was cool. Most of the guys hit the crossbar or missed the net, but I'll take it."

Kyle Konin

The Tampa Bay Lightning winning the Stanley Cup in 2004 helped plenty of people in the area and around Florida become hockey fans. Their decline in the few years after started Kyle Konin's path to the NHL, even if only for a day.

Konin was six when he and his family moved from Rhode Island to the Tampa area, the same year the Lightning hoisted the Cup before the lockout wiped out the 2004–05 NHL season. The Lightning were out of the playoffs by coach John Tortorella's final season in 2007–08 and the next year were one of the league's worst teams. That made it possible for Kyle and younger brother Chris to get tickets for $10.

"Me and my brother got hooked into hockey from just going to Lightning games," Kyle said. "We kind of got spoiled because we were able to go to so many games because it was so affordable. We just started playing in the street—road hockey and roller hockey."

Konin credits the likes of Karri Ramo, Johan Holmqvist, and Mike Smith for turning him into a goaltender.

"The Lightning goalie was really the only one who would ever do anything great," he said. "He was getting peppered every game, so if they ever won a game, it was because he stood on his head. I think I just kind of fell in love with the sport and goaltending at the same time."

After spending much of his childhood in Clearwater, Florida, Konin played travel hockey back in Rhode Island as a teenager and then attended Kimball Union Academy in New Hampshire, at the same time turning his hobby of painting goalie masks into a profitable venture on the side and in the summer.

He played Tier 3 junior hockey with the Atlanta Capitals of the North American 3 Hockey League, made a short stop in Topeka, Kansas, and moved on to play in the Eastern Hockey League for the New Hampshire Avalanche and Vermont Lumberjacks. Konin played club hockey at Grand Valley State University in Michigan before moving back to the Tampa area.

Konin began skating at Xtra Ice rink in Tampa with a handful of former NHL players, including goaltenders Dwayne Roloson and Mathieu Garon, plus defenseman Filip Kuba, whom he watched play for the Lightning in the mid to late 2000s. The warehouse converted to a hockey rink has a 140-by-65 foot "micro" surface smaller than the NHL-sized 200-by-85 dimensions, but getting on the ice there got him in touch with the Lightning through Garon. When the emergency backup goaltender program restarted in the fall of 2021, Konin was on Tampa Bay's list.

It was Thursday, December 2, the morning after Jett Alexander dressed for warm-ups as Colorado's backup at Toronto, and Konin was on the ice with Roloson, Garon, Kuba, and Co. He had Lightning general manager Julien BriseBois' contact information but didn't talk to him regularly, so Konin knew something was up when he stepped off the ice at 11 AM to see a couple of missed calls from him.

The St. Louis Blues were in town, and 2019 Stanley Cup–winning goaltender Jordan Binnington had tested positive for the novel coronavirus and gone on the NHL's COVID protocol list. With a handful of short-term injuries already stretching them, the Blues did not have the salary cap space to call up a goalie from the minors, so GM Doug Armstrong asked BriseBois for his local EBUG of the day. BriseBois explained the situation to Konin, who waited for a call from a St. Louis area code.

Konin told Armstrong and coach Craig Berube he'd had a nice skate with his beer league guys and was ready to go. He got razzed the next week for referring to former NHL players as beer-leaguers, but the Blues were just happy to have someone to back up Ville Husso for the night.

After Armstrong announced Binnington was out and the team would be using an EBUG, he was asked what the goalie's name was. He pulled out his phone and read, "Kyle Konin—K-o-n-i-n. You can do Google research on him."

"We're excited to have him in here," Armstrong added. "Knock on wood that he'll remain a 60-minute cheerleader."

The rest of Konin's day became a blur. He made his arrangements with the Blues, told family and friends the news that he'd be dressing in an NHL game, and returned home, where he dried out his gear, printed out and signed the amateur tryout contract, and tied up some loose ends before driving to Amalie Arena. After arriving carrying his blue-and-white Lightning-themed gear, he found a KONIN 31 Blues jersey hanging in his locker stall. He took part in the Blues' pregame soccer activity—a popular hockey ritual—and got the full experience as though he were actually in the NHL.

Players treated him like that, too. Konin stood at the back of the line of players to step on the ice for warm-ups, but Vladimir Tarasenko and Ryan O'Reilly were having none of it. They sent him to the front of the line to take a solo lap around the ice before anyone else went out there: an NHL tradition for a rookie making his debut. Brayden Schenn made Konin take off his mask for the full effect.

"I would have never done that, especially because I've been trying to grow my hair out and it's at kind of the awkward stage right now. It doesn't lay down perfectly so it's kind of the in-between stage," Konin said a week later. "I was like, 'Well, you at least got to let me wear a hat out there or something.' They're like, 'Nope, no bucket, no nothing, you're going.'"

Konin stepped on to the ice at the same time as star Lightning goalie Andrei Vasilevskiy and took his no-helmet lap before being joined by the rest of the Blues.

"The nerves were really going, and I was the only one out there," he said. "That's when I was a little nervous about losing an edge or something."

Konin was used to skating at Amalie Arena for Lightning practices and morning skates, but it was different this time with fans in the building.

"That's something I've always dreamed about doing, and it was just like my dream coming true," he said.

Konin caught up with Tampa Bay backup Brian Elliott, whom he hadn't seen since the last time he skated with the Lightning. And he attempted to stay out of the way of Blues players, who tried to keep him updated on what drill was coming next. He saw 13 shots in net and took four himself into the empty cage.

Much like Alex Bishop in Toronto, Konin got to sit on the bench and take in the whole game while Husso started.

"Just to experience everything at that level was incredible," Konin said. "Not that I accomplished by any means what those guys have, but to get to live it out for that one day and to get treated like I did, it was crazy."

Husso was actually injured in the Blues' next game two days later at the Florida Panthers, and by then they had called up Charlie Lindgren from the American Hockey League. Konin returned to Xtra Ice for more sessions with his now fellow NHL alumni and went back to work at NuJax, where he airbrushes goalie masks for a living.

"I get to work with some established hockey players, some beer-league hockey players," he said. "I've always had a huge passion for hockey, and I want to stay around the game as long as I can, whether it's playing or coaching or working. It fits right into that."

Dustin Smith

After moving to Nashville from San Diego at age 10, Dustin Smith did not need ice to fall in love with hockey. He had seen *The Mighty Ducks* movies earlier in the '90s and began playing in a coach's backyard with an old baseball glove and tennis balls. That was enough to make him a goalie.

Smith tended goal in high school and then played college club hockey at Middle Tennessee State from 2006 to '09. That was it as far as competitive hockey, as Smith moved on to beer league games until an opportunity presented itself in the fall of 2012.

The NHL was at the beginning of another lockout, so the Predators players in the area in need of a goalie to shoot on invited Smith to practice with them. Smith became a go-to Nashville practice goalie, skating with players as part of informal summer workouts and occasionally during the season. He began working for Southwest Airlines at the Nashville airport.

Smith was the co-winner of the Florida Panthers emergency backup goaltender tryout in March 2015 and took the full-time position with the Predators as soon as the league program began. He had a close call on January 12, 2017, when the Boston Bruins were in town and Tukka Rask took a puck to the throat on a slap shot from Predators defenseman Roman Josi during the first period. Smith joked to a team staffer that he was in the building in case he was needed, and at intermission he was told to get down to the locker room and get dressed.

He attended games over several seasons without another sniff. Watching Scott Foster and Ayres play so well after going in as EBUGs inspired Smith when he was back at it following the shutdown.

"I was getting kind of complacent where it was just going to all these games and nothing really happening and I got comfortable just going to hang out at the games," he said. "It's tough to really kind of take everything too seriously because you go to so many games and nothing happens, but after everything with Scott Foster and David Ayres, going into this year I really kind of wanted to take things I guess a little more seriously."

Smith had a day off from marshaling planes and driving bags around the tarmac on December 16, 2021. He tried to make sure he wasn't working his day job when he was scheduled as an emergency backup and even began a game day routine of stretching and doing some Sense Arena virtual reality goaltending training. He had just finished that routine when the call came that a bunch of Avalanche players had tested positive for the novel coronavirus and they needed another goalie for the night.

It was 90 minutes until puck drop and an hour before warm-ups when Smith was told, "We need you to come down here as fast as you can." He packed a bag, made the drive downtown, got dressed, and took warm-ups with Colorado. He served as Pavel Francouz's backup and felt reinvigorated by the chance.

"Everything happened really quick," Smith said "I was super nervous right away. But I think this year kind of having the refreshed mentality of expecting to have something happen, the nervousness quickly turned into excitement. Taking that break kind of helped me get more in the mindset of being, I guess, a little more serious with it."

The Avalanche calling on Smith only validated Keefe's feeling earlier in the season that his Maple Leafs wouldn't be the last team to dress an EBUG given the salary cap and other roster restrictions made more difficult by pandemic protocols.

"It's an unfortunate situation that's a reality of the flat cap system here," Keefe said. "You're going to see a lot of that throughout the league."

CHAPTER 15

THE VICTORY LAP: GOALIES CELEBRATED FOR STEPPING IN

JORGE ALVES did not expect all the mail.

The Carolina Hurricanes equipment manager got into an NHL game for 7.6 seconds on New Year's Eve 2016, and five years later he was still receiving packages at his house from all over the world. Hockey cards or pictures of him to autograph, sometimes first responder patches as a tribute to the Marine Corps veteran who had a sip of coffee in the show.

"The story inspired them or whatever," Alves said. "It's really interesting and humbling at the same time because you're like, 'Oh man, this is crazy.'"

Scott Foster and David Ayres know all about the craziness that comes with entering a game as an emergency backup goaltender. The pieces of mail, sometimes with specific instructions to sign with a certain color marker, are still arriving years after Foster's game in Chicago in 2018 and Ayres' game in 2020. Foster started getting fan mail, letters—even jerseys to sign—at his home and office.

"All these things and nothing related to work whatsoever: photos, cards, pucks," he said. "At this point I realize it's just a byproduct of what happened."

Before Foster became a Blackhawks folk hero for his 14 minutes of NHL action, the team had another EBUG to honor.

When starter Corey Crawford needed an emergency appendectomy on the morning of an afternoon game at Philadelphia in December 2016, former Temple University club goalie Eric Semborski got a round of applause from players when he arrived in the locker room just before warm-ups. Even though he only took warm-ups and backed up Scott Darling that day, the Blackhawks invited Semborski to Chicago for a game eight days later to tour the locker room and make an appearance in front of fans on the video boards inside the United Center. Darling reached out to Semborski to extend the invite to him and his wife, Kaitlyn. They landed on one of the final flights that got into Chicago before a snowstorm canceled many more.

Semborski had never been to Chicago before that. Just over a week after dressing for the Blackhawks, he was the guest of honor getting a standing ovation from the crowd of 21,451. He was recognized while walking around the concourse by fans who knew his name and asked for photos and autographs. Semborski had signed some autographs after Temple games, "but nothing like this," he said.

Semborski caught up with some of his one-day teammates and played Xbox with Patrick Kane that night after the Blackhawks' game against Dallas. When the Blackhawks returned to Philadelphia nearly a year later, Semborski met up with them again. After putting his red game jersey from 2016—really Crawford's with the No. 50 on it and a Semborski nameplate—through the laundry afterward, the team sent it back to him to keep.

It's hanging in a closet at his house with other hockey jerseys.

———————

Foster did not expect his NHL appearance to blow up as much as it did. The accountant by day and Blackhawks goaltender by night conceded later that might have been naïve for him to think given how quickly his 14 minutes of game action went viral. Before leaving the arena that night, he had to figure something out. Chicago's VP of communications, Adam Rogowin, knew how big the story was getting and asked Foster how he wanted to proceed from there.

"I'm good," Foster told him. "I'm done."

Foster thought at the time there wasn't anything more he could add to the story, so he told the Blackhawks they could respectfully decline any interview requests. He said the same to his company, Golub Capital. Of course, that didn't stop them from piling up for the team, at Johnny's IceHouse where he plays beer league, at Foster's office on every phone and email address imaginable, and even at his family's house in Oak Park, Illinois.

He returned home from work the day after the game to find that news crews had been on the front lawn. But even on the train back from downtown Chicago, Foster was hyper-focused on the conversations around him and the extra glance or two knowing he was in the news.

"It was not the same," he said. "I did not feel the same."

Foster enjoyed a few hours of celebration Friday night, 24 hours after his game, with an inner circle of friends and family, but the calls and messages snowballed through the weekend and into Monday. He didn't think he'd need help navigating the attention and aftermath of making seven saves in an NHL game, but once he asked for it, everything became easier. Foster picked his spots and said yes "mostly when it felt fun."

It doesn't get much more fun than Las Vegas, so Foster accepted the league's invitation to its annual awards show there in June. He and his wife, Erin, had never been to Las Vegas before, and they got to get their photo taken on the red carpet before the show. Foster was a co-presenter of the Vezina Trophy for top goaltender along with actor Jim Belushi.

"Hockey is the only sport where anybody can literally suit up and play on any given night," Belushi said on stage before introducing Foster. "I know it sounds like something out of a movie, but this year in Chicago, it really happened."

Belushi called Foster "Johnny H&R Block"—despite the fact that none of his job as an accountant involves taxes—and Foster said he had to make this quick and get back to work.

"Work. Great," Belushi said. "Any advice for any of these kids out there who dream of following in your footsteps?"

"Yeah, I sure do," Foster responded. "First I'd suggest a major in accounting with a master's in accountancy."

Foster was beginning to enjoy it and agreed to attend the Blackhawks fan convention in late July at the Hilton Chicago. He did an emergency goaltender panel with broadcaster Pat Foley, goaltending coach Jimmy Waite, equipment manager Troy Parchman, and retired-goalie-turned-team executive Mark Bernard and signed plenty of autographs. His parents, in-laws, wife, daughters, and other family members and friends were on hand for the weekend.

When the festivities were over, Scott and Erin stayed in the city to have a nice dinner Saturday night. As they tried to make their way through the lobby to leave the hotel, Foster was approached by fans asking for photos and autographs. A line formed, and he signed as much as he could until it was time to go. Only problem was, he had a pile of gifts and keepsakes fans gave him that he couldn't exactly carry around the streets of Chicago. He and Erin made a plan that he would hang out in a corner while she took the elevator back to their room to drop off the stuff.

On her way back down to the lobby, Erin was in the elevator with a young boy and his parents who were there for the convention. She asked the boy if he had gotten all the autographs he wanted. All except one, he said: Scott Foster. They got to the bottom.

"Come with me," she said, walking the boy over to Scott. They chatted for a bit, his parents offered their appreciation, and Scott and Erin left the hotel out the back door to make their reservation on time.

While walking down Michigan Avenue, Foster heard his name being yelled. It was the boy who wanted his autograph and, in the excitement of the moment, had forgotten to ask him to sign his replica Blackhawks mask. There's only one other signature on it: Corey Crawford's.

"Absolutely," Foster said, adding his name to the mask.

This is cool for me, Foster thought to himself. *Just a wickedly good goalie and human being and this kid wants me on that mask? I'll do this 100 times if you want me to. It's the coolest moment.*

There have been plenty of moments in the years since in which Foster gets recognized. Sometimes it's on the concourse at United Center when he takes his family to a game as fans. Sometimes it's when he's picking up or dropping off his daughters at school. In the fall of 2021, he had to clear up a misconception when a mother of one of his youngest daughter's kindergarten friends said her son kept coming home mentioning, "Wynni's dad plays for the Blackhawks."

"Well, *played*," Foster said. "One time. Fourteen minutes. Like, yes and no."

Around adults at work, Foster has had clients ask for the extra handshake or photo. "That wasn't happening on March 28," he said. He also sent the president of Golub Capital a signed jersey as a thank you for the company's support. Foster said the company had T-shirts printed for employees with a goalie silhouette, his Blackhawks No. 90, and the message, "Keep calm and let our goalie handle it."

Instead of Clark Kent ditching the suit for the Superman cape, Foster every once in a while can be the emergency goalie and then resume his everyday roles as a father, husband, and accountant.

"It can't affect it too much, or it's a problem," he said. "It's weird that it's a subset of your life that you then kind of enter back into. It's compartmentalized as part of my regular life."

Foster can go to some Blackhawks games as a fan without getting recognized. The odd time getting a beer on the 300 level he'd have someone approach to say, "I was at your game."

It's still fun for him when friends, family, or folks from the Blackhawks see FOSTER 90 jerseys and snap a quick photo to send along. And his daughters have no problem wearing custom T-shirts to games at United Center.

"It's still a little bit of a unicorn," Foster said of seeing fans wear his jersey in the wild. "Probably everyone in my family owns one at this point."

Foster was not honored by the team during a game as quickly as Semborski because their final home date in the spring of 2018 conflicted with one of his leagues at Johnny's IceHouse. That Friday night in April, Foster remembers declining all interview requests but also fans streaming over from United Center when the Blackhawks were done to watch him play a game that started at 9:40 PM.

When he was a spectator the following season, the team got a suite for Foster and his family to attend a game. He got a video tribute and a standing ovation from fans when he was shown on arena video screens and "did the awkward wave to the crowd."

"It's weird because it's referred to as, 'That Scott Foster game,'" he said. "It was really Brent Seabrook Night. It's very strange that this date was like your thing. I was supposed to be playing at Johnny's that night."

Well aware of that tale of missing a beer league game to dress and play in the NHL, Phil Pritchard from the Hockey Hall of Fame reached out and had a very specific request. He wanted Foster's beer league jerseys. Foster agreed right away and sent a letter to Pritchard explaining which team's jersey he was supposed to be wearing on the night of March 29, 2018.

Foster continued wearing his NHL gear until early 2020 and retired it to his basement. The pads, blocker, and gloves are rigged up well off the ground to keep them from getting damaged by any water that gets in.

"This might be my kids' inheritance," he said. "They're bulky to store, but I don't think I could ever part ways with it. I'll let my kids fight over left pad, right pad, glove, blocker."

He has a framed FOSTER 90 Blackhawks jersey hanging up in his house, signed by all the players who were part of his game. That was a gift from the Blackhawks. Because he signed an amateur contract, he wasn't paid a dime for playing in the game but walked away with his jersey.

"Nothing but the jersey," he said. "I don't need 500 bucks. You can pry that jersey out of my cold, dead hands."

That game-worn jersey made a trip over the border back to Canada for a family event. Foster said he was "sweating buckets" when people wanted to put it on for photos.

"All the marks are game marks—they're puck marks," he said. "Those are stops that I made in the NHL that somehow I pulled that off. Those are real. Those are mine."

Where is it now? Back on a hanger in Foster's closet.

"I'll put it behind glass eventually," he said. "It probably is on the same to-do list I've had about my college jersey. It's in my closet and it nearly never comes out of there because it's odd that you'd hang it framed up because it means something special, but it also doesn't come out of the closet because it means something special. And I don't want people touching it."

———————

The circus started to form before Ayres was finished winning a game for the Hurricanes against his hometown Maple Leafs. He was the first emergency backup goaltender to win an NHL game, and it was all happening on a Saturday night in February in Toronto, under hockey's biggest spotlight. Carolina director of communications Pace Sagester used the margins of his second intermission stat sheet to jot down all the postgame requests for Ayres, from the Canadian national television broadcast to the dozens of writers in the building.

The moment Ayres stepped off the ice as the first star of the game, Sagester told him to stick by him and he'd guide him through the process. Little did either of them know at the time how much of a process there would be.

Ayres' first interview with Kyle Bukauskas came with the famous *Hockey Night in Canada* towel wrapped around his shoulders. For an Ontario kid who grew up a hockey fan, that itself was an accomplishment. But it was only the start. He did a handful of other appearances before leaving the rink that night and practiced with the American Hockey League's Toronto Marlies on Sunday morning like nothing had changed.

Of course, everything had changed. Ayres was the biggest story in sports, let alone hockey, and the Hurricanes invited him to Raleigh for their home game the following Tuesday to give their new hero a proper welcome. First, though, the team was getting inundated with outside requests. Ayres agreed to first fly to New York City for a media tour. VP of communications

Mike Sundheim had to stay back for the NHL trade deadline Monday, so he called Sagester on a couple of hours' notice and told him his flight was booked and he was accompanying Ayres to New York.

They met up Sunday night at an Irish pub. A day and a half earlier, they didn't know each other existed and the world had not been introduced to the Zamboni driver and arena manager who saved the day by entering an NHL game in goal.

"We were just trying to wrap our head around everything that was going on," Sagester said.

The car picked them up at the JW Marriott Essex House just after 6 AM Monday and whisked them off to Rockefeller center for the *TODAY* show on NBC. Ayres met Al Roker, spent time in the green room, and took his place in Studio 1A. Ayres talked about his 2004 kidney transplant from his mother, Mary, and was asked if he had spoken to her since the game Saturday night.

"Barely," Ayres responded. "She keeps texting me and I'm so busy that I feel bad I'm not really answering her."

Mary joined the show by video from her home: "Hi, son!"

"David, you know what, I always was very proud of you from the beginning," she said. "This has just made me so extremely proud. I have no words. I couldn't sleep for the first night. Your dad and I always said you would get where you are today."

"Come on, Mom," David said, wiping tears from his eyes.

It was the most emotional part of Ayres' day, but it certainly wasn't his final stop. Ayres did several radio and TV call-ins and joined *Fox & Friends* before lunch. With a film crew following every step of the way, he went to the NHL offices and met with Commissioner Gary Bettman before doing *NBC Nightly News*.

"This is how it's going to be all day," Sagester told Ayres. "Let me know when you're tired."

With *NBC Nightly News* the last thing left on tap, Sagester got a call from NHL senior director of corporate communications Nirva Milord, who had been contacted by producers for *The Late Show with Stephen Colbert*. CBS was willing to pay to change their flights if Ayres would join the show.

"Dave, you've done so much today," Sagester said. "This is totally up to you. But Colbert's the No. 1 nightly show in the U.S. It's a big deal. He wants you on the show. If you're not wanting to do it, we'll take our normal flight. If you are, we're not going to be able to get back to Raleigh until midnight and you have a big day tomorrow."

Without hesitation, Ayres agreed. He nailed the rehearsals, and his Colbert appearance featured plenty of emergency fill-in bits.

"We got a great show for you tonight—oww, oh, God, I pulled my hamstring!" Colbert said. "I don't think I can finish the monologue."

Ayres sprinted on stage in his Hurricanes uniform. "Don't worry, Stephen, I got you!"

"It's Zamboni hockey hero, David Ayres, everybody!" Colbert said to a round of applause. "David, I pulled my hamstring. Can you help me out?"

"Oh, I'll finish it up for you. We got a great show for you tonight. When we get back, Warren checks Bloomberg into the boards, so stick around!"

Two days after Hurricanes players sprayed water bottles all over Ayres when he walked into the visiting locker room following the game, Colbert doused him with water on stage. Coming out of a commercial, Ayres had replaced Jon Batiste at the piano, playing with his glove and blocker on.

"Hey, Stephen. Jon got hurt, so I'm in now," Ayres said.

Ayres was a star across North America for his 28 minutes of NHL action, and nowhere was he more beloved than in Raleigh, North Carolina. Mayor Mary-Ann Baldwin declared Tuesday, February 25, 2020, David Ayres Day in the city. He spent the day doing local TV appearances.

"He was an instant celebrity in our marketplace," Hurricanes general manager Don Waddell said. "Everybody wanted to talk with him."

As new local celebrities, David and Sarah Ayres couldn't go anywhere in Raleigh without being recognized.

"I had to put my hood on and my hat on, and we tried to go to the mall and Sarah and I got spotted," Ayres said. "Probably three or four steps into the mall, someone's yelling my name, and you couldn't really go anywhere because everybody noticed who you were the whole time. They were great, and the fan base loved it. It just goes to show how dedicated their fan base is."

When he got to PNC Arena, he had one more radio appearance and did it while sitting on the steps outside before going in for the game. A crowd of 50 or so fans formed around him and cheered as soon as he hung up the phone. He signed autographs and took pictures with as many as he could.

"People light up when they see you," Sarah Ayres said about the reception she and David get in Raleigh. "It's the greatest thing to be walking and somebody recognizes him, and they get a smile on their face. It's not even for what it does for him. It's just seeing that interaction."

David fired up the crowd before that game by manning the arena siren and did so again in the 2021 playoffs and early the next season, the first time the Hurricanes played the Maple Leafs again since February. He was described on arena video screens as "Hurricanes alum and legendary goaltender Dave Ayres" and "Canes EBUG Legend."

"If there's a team that gets it, it's us," Carolina coach Rod Brind'Amour said. "We're also an entertainment sport. We've got to sell the game down here, especially, and whether it's a novelty, whether it's something a little different that creates a little buzz and a story, we're going to jump on it."

The Hurricanes began selling AYRES 90 T-shirts at their arena store and online. The proceeds from that and arena sales of R&D Brewing's Storm Brew beer sold that night went to the National Kidney Foundation. David and Sarah also teamed up with the Logan Boulet Effect promoting organ donation in the name of the 16-year-old Humboldt Broncos junior hockey player who was killed in the team's 2018 bus crash.

"If we can get just a few people signing organ donation cards and get some sort of focus on that, that's all it takes," Sarah Ayres said, hoping David's story can be an inspiration. "This is a positive story and it's happy. People can be upset that it happened. People can go on about the 15 minutes of fame, but the truth is it's a fantastic story. Everything that comes out of it when people talk to you is positive."

Sagester, who now works at the University of North Carolina, said the Hurricanes couldn't have gotten luckier that it was Ayres' turn to be the EBUG in Toronto.

"He had the best outlook and attitude the whole time because he was aware of the situation he was in," he said. "I was blown away. And after all that, I went from, 'I'll never see this guy again' to 'I've got a friend for life.'"

Later in the week, Ayres returned to Toronto and donated his Carolina–Toronto game-used stick to the Hockey Hall of Fame.

"I didn't expect all of this. I expected to go on the ice and play a couple of minutes and get off and maybe do one or two interviews," Ayres said at the Hall of Fame. "Haven't really had a chance to have it all sink in."

The pandemic shutting down the 2019–20 season in March brought the victory lap to a screeching halt. But there was still a long-lasting appreciation for just how bizarre Ayres' journey from a kidney transplant to one game in the NHL at age 42 actually was.

"This is something that I don't know if anybody could ever dream how this all turned out," Waddell said. "You put the whole story together, and I don't know if you could ever write a better script."

James Corden's production company signed on to make a script of Ayres' story to become a Disney movie. After getting a handful of pitches, Ayres signed on with Creative Artists Agency and ultimately chose Corden to work on the project.

"It was surreal because our kids love him," Ayres told the Hurricanes website. "Our daughter thinks he's unbelievably hysterical and when I came home and told her, she said, 'Like, the real James Corden?' She was super pumped about it."

After so much concern behind the scenes that Ayres was going to get lit up by the Maple Leafs, Alves said, "All in all, it turned into a Disney movie."

At home in Bowmanville, Ontario, David and Sarah made a stall on the ground floor to hold his goaltending gear because he was tired of dragging it to the basement. It's now a shrine to his appearance with the Hurricanes.

But his actual game jersey? It's still hanging in the closet.

"Sarah keeps bugging me to get it framed," Ayres said. "I'm like, 'What if I ever need it? What if I ever have to pull it out for anything?'"

Just in case he is ever needed to play in the NHL one more time.

CHAPTER 16

EBUGS OF THE FUTURE: WHAT'S IN STORE FOR HOCKEY'S ONE-DAY JOB?

W HEN DAVID AYRES ALLOWED GOALS on the first two shots he faced as the Carolina Hurricanes' emergency backup goaltender against the Toronto Maple Leafs in February 2020, the complaints and debate began. How could the greatest hockey league in the world let a goaltender who doesn't play in the NHL play such a big role in an important game in the middle of a playoff race?

Even after Ayres stopped the next eight Maple Leafs shots and became, as Stephen Colbert put it, a "Zamboni hockey hero," the conversation roared on. Many across the sport argued there had to be a better system for the rare occasion when a team loses two goaltenders to injury.

"I think we could probably come up with a better solution than an EBUG," retired goaltender Roberto Luongo said. "It's a cool story when you see it. It's awesome. That one turned out OK, but sometimes these situations might not."

When the league's general managers convened a little over a week later, they decided to keep things the way they were.

"It's such a rare occurrence. It's only news because it recently happened," Vegas Golden Knights GM Kelly McCrimmon said at the time. "We're comfortable with the way that it is."

Scott Foster in 2018, Ayres in 2020, and Tom Hodges in 2022 were the only emergency backup goaltenders to see meaningful action in a game since the NHL instituted the two-goalie system in 1965. But the game has changed; skaters are following through on coaches preaching to "crash the net," and more injuries are happening to the masked men in the crease.

"The league's faster," Florida Panthers goaltending coach Robb Tallas said. "Guys are handling quite a big workload, so to have an injury or multiple injuries happen in a game, it has happened now, and it's come up more often than we would like."

When each NHL team had a third goalie around on a taxi squad during the pandemic-shortened 2021 season, day-of and in-game injuries were less of an immediate concern because there was always another option.

Deputy Commissioner Bill Daly said the EBUG situation is a "constant focus" for the league. With concussions and other injuries to goalies a stark reality and even salary cap problems that prevent recalling someone from the minors, there is a hot debate to be had about the future of the most unique position in sports and no shortage of ideas.

Status Quo

Ayres was much more of the exception than the rule as a 42-year-old arena operator stepping in. Toronto's emergency backup goaltenders mostly come from the University of Toronto, Ryerson University, and York University, and he would like to see them continue getting opportunities.

"I think it's cool. I'm kind of hoping they stick with it," Ayres said. "Even if the guys don't get in the games, these university kids get to go to these games, which actually is going to force them in their university games and practices to keep getting better and better and better. It kind of shows, who knows where you can go? Who knows what's going to happen to you in a few years or any day now when you're at a Leaf game and you're the emergency guy?"

Count one more vote for more of the same from Anaheim Ducks goaltender Anthony Stolarz, who spent the 2021 season on the taxi squad and whose injury in April 2022 paved the way for Hodges' appearance. He thinks keeping three goalies around is a hindrance to development and enjoys the rare chance to watch unheralded players get in uniform and sometimes on the ice.

"The guys who never had a chance at thinking they'd play in the NHL, it gives them an opportunity to at least sit on the bench, be around the guys, kind of see what it's like," Stolarz said. "I just like the uniqueness of the EBUG. It's something that you don't ever see, and the odds of someone going in are very limited. But you look at the stories like Foster and Ayres and it makes for great TV, and you see stuff like that, you can only smile at it."

Alex Bishop, who got to dress for the Maple Leafs and watch University of Toronto teammate and housemate Jett Alexander take warm-ups for the Colorado Avalanche, selfishly wants to keep the same system so similar goalies can experience what he did. But he also sees the other side of it that NHL teams might not want to rely on someone who's not at that level of play.

"I would imagine something's going to be done about it eventually, but I hope not," Bishop said.

Three-Goalie System

The easiest way to make sure there's always an NHL-caliber goaltender available is to have an extra one available nearby.

Absent the Ottawa Senators domino effect of injuries that almost put forward Artem Anisimov in net, the taxi squads of 2021 provided a safe backup plan.

But the safest option is also the least popular. Three's a crowd on a sheet of ice with two nets.

"Practicing with three goalies, it's no good," Foster said. "You need games. It's hard on those guys. There's not enough reps. There's not enough practice time, especially when the schedule gets long and you're on the road."

Stolarz found this out the hard way in 2021 as the third option behind John Gibson and Ryan Miller, appearing in just eight games with Anaheim and three more with the American Hockey League's San Diego Gulls.

"You want your third goalie to be playing someplace," Carolina Hurricanes general manager Don Waddell said. "[The 2021 season] was hard on the taxi goalies. Some goalies never played hardly any games at all. And that's not good for their development or their career, either."

The taxi squad allowed teams to continue paying players as though they were in the minors and not count against the salary cap. The cap ramifications of keeping a third goalie essentially rules out the possibility unless an exception is written into the rules.

Justin Goldman, founder of The Goalie Guild nonprofit foundation and a former Denver-based emergency backup, has had conversations with others working internationally in the business about hockey teams expanding beyond the current two-goalie setup regularly.

"We are now starting to wonder, why are there only two goalies on a team?" Goldman said. "You have five pitchers in a rotation. You've got three quarterbacks on a roster. Why in God's name at this point do we only have two goalies on a roster? It just doesn't make sense anymore. The game has changed so much."

Minor League Rotation

Tallas, Luongo, and others around the sport have gravitated toward a hybrid solution. Each team would carry a third goalie at all times off the salary cap but only for a certain amount of time, be it games or weeks.

"He's coming up as an emergency, he's practicing with the team, he's traveling with the team, he's getting NHL experience with the team and then after his time of two weeks being up, he goes back down and then maybe you call your other guy up and kind of revolve that door so they're getting the experience," Tallas said. "The younger guys are getting the experience of coming up. When one guy's up, the other guy's getting a little bit more playing time, so it's working out for the goalies in the minors."

Tallas said other goalie coaches around the league are in favor of the revolving door concept because it would mean using prospects in the system in the event of an emergency rather than someone they've never worked with before.

Peter Luukko, who became facilities chairman at Oak View Group (the development company behind the Seattle Kraken's Climate Pledge Arena), was convinced by Tallas during his time with the Panthers about the rotation idea, perhaps in five-game segments.

"Why not give a kid a chance that's in your system and you're possibly looking into the future for?" he said. "It's a league of professionals and the more you can involve professionals, the better off the league is for it."

Practice Goalies

Retired goaltender Mike McKenna has suggested each team carrying a full-time third goalie who travels and is available for practices and in emergency situations. In a column for Daily

Faceoff, McKenna wondered if the cap shouldn't be set at a salary of $250,000 to even the playing field around the league but make sure everyone has an NHL-caliber option just in case.

"When I finished two seasons ago, if a team had offered me $150k (plus per diem) to eat pucks, stay at the Ritz, and fly charter around North America eating filet mignon I would have signed in a heartbeat," McKenna wrote. "I don't think I would have done it for more than a season or two, but it would have been a great way to wind down my career without having to deal with the performance anxiety associated with regular starts."

The NHL Players' Association might have something to say about keeping around a professional for a third of the league minimum who doesn't count against the salary cap or the roster. But other adaptations of McKenna's theories are out there, including taking the current crop of amateur EBUGs and turning it into a paying, traveling gig that's more than just being on call.

Goldman believes something has to give because the demands on goalies are so high physically, mentally, and emotionally.

"You pay a guy to basically be your target practice and your emergency backup goalie and your assistant video coordinator or some kind of role in the team," Goldman said. "But he's also that guy because there's just too many guys getting injured, whether it's in a game or it's in practice or it's long term or it's just some fluke accident. It's too important of a role now. You better have someone that can step in."

Women's Goalies

When Nicole Hensley and Shannon Szabados were goaltending for the Buffalo Beauts of the National Women's Hockey League, agent Brant Feldman had an idea for Sabres GM Jason Botterill coming out of the 2018 Winter Olympics in Pyeongchang: Why not use women's goalies as emergency backups? Botterill liked the idea, but it did not catch on at the time.

Feldman said the height of women's goalies might be questioned compared to modern-day men at the position but asked, "What's the difference between that and an accountant from Chicago getting to play or a Zamboni driver from Toronto?"

"The women are in better shape, in better nutritional shape" than some EBUGs, Feldman said. "I thought to myself, this could be good, and the women would have as much reps as anyone else."

It remains an intriguing possibility, decades after women's star Manon Rheaume appeared in exhibition games for the Tampa Bay Lightning in 1992 and 1993. More recently, Szabados, who won two Olympic medals with Canada, played against men in the Southern Professional Hockey League, and the growth of the women's game could allow for more than a dozen goalies to serve as EBUGs on any given night.

"If you were going to put a clock on me or a timetable of, 'When are we going to see it?' I don't know," said ESPN's Linda Cohn, who was a goaltender in high school and college. "There's so many qualified male goalies out there who are looking for an opportunity to shine. There's so many guys in waiting. But would these women be capable of doing so in an emergency backup situation? Yes, and it would not be a publicity stunt. It's because they're more than capable."

One of the biggest joys Foster got in the aftermath of his 14-minute appearance for the Chicago Blackhawks was youngest daughter Wynnifred taking up hockey. There's certainly no guarantee she'll grow up to be a goalie like her dad, but he's a big supporter of women's players taking over EBUG spots.

"I don't know why if it's not a conversation that's being had, shouldn't already be had," Foster said. "I don't know what the barrier would be. This is putting me in my place real quick, but any one of those players that's playing at that level has to be better than me.

"It makes sense to me that would be a great way. If you're concerned about the quality of an EBUG, that is a great way to start addressing that."

ACKNOWLEDGMENTS

THE WRITING OF THIS BOOK would not have been possible without the support of many friends, colleagues, and family members.

I met Ben Raby for the first time in the Washington Capitals media room in 2011 when I started covering the team for the *Washington Times*. He came away with the first impression of, "Who the hell is this guy?" We quickly became friends. I was honored to attend his wedding, and he put me in touch with the folks at Triumph Books when I had a crazy idea to write about emergency backup goaltenders. He's forgotten more about hockey than I've ever known.

Thank you to Bill Ames and Michelle Bruton at Triumph for making this book possible. I was a little surprised no one thought of doing it before, after Scott Foster and David Ayres captivated the hockey community by playing goal in the NHL despite not actually being in the NHL.

But the everyman stories started way before a Chicago accountant went in net for the Blackhawks. That's why I owe thanks to longtime Associated Press deputy sports editor Howie Rumberg, who came up with the idea for a story on EBUGs back in January 2017. Carolina Hurricanes equipment manager Jorge Alves had just played 7.6 seconds at the end of a game, and it got him thinking. After talking to old-school emergency backup goalies like Tom Fenton and Nathan Schoenfeld, I had a story that won an Associated Press Sports Editors award for best feature.

Professionally, I believe in something my dad has said often—it's better to be lucky than good. Bosses like Mike Harris, Julie Scott, Dave Zelio, Oscar Dixon, and Michael Giarrusso took a chance by hiring me. Julie in particular, since she hired an American kid to cover hockey in Canada for the Canadian Press. I hope I didn't disappoint any of you.

Some of the most important people in my life I've met through this crazy business of hockey writing: Dave Isaac, Brian McNally, Zac Boyer, Scott Burnside, Chris Johnston, Mike Zeisberger, Kevin McGran, Ken Wiebe, Katie Brown, Pam Chvotkin, and so many others who were there with a phone number, a careful read, a piece of advice, or just a conversation to keep me on the rails throughout the book-writing process.

Of course, the stories in this book aren't mine. They belong to Alves, Foster, Ayres, Fenton, Schoenfeld, Tom Hodges, Carter Hutton, and all the EBUGs who were gracious with their time and energy no matter how annoying the requests got. The project reminded me of one of the best things about hockey and hockey players—it's a small town full of regular people who are quick to introduce themselves even though you already know who they are. It would've been an even more challenging endeavor without the cooperation and help from so many people around hockey.

Finally, thank you to my parents, Donna and John, and my brother, Chris, mostly for putting up with me. As Ben knows, it's not easy.

SOURCES

Books

Conner, Floyd. *Hockey's Most Wanted: The Top 10 Book of Wicked Slapshots, Bruising Goons and Ice Oddities* (Dulles, Virginia: Potomac Books, 2002).

Cude, Wilfred: *Dear Red Light: Some Seasons in the Life of a NHL Goalkeeper* (Mary-Pat Cude, 2021).

National Hockey League Official Guide & Record Book (Chicago, Illinois: Triumph Books, 2015).

Podnieks, Andrew. *Players: The Ultimate A-Z Guide of Everyone Who Has Ever Played in the NHL* (Toronto, Ontario: Doubleday Canada, 2003).

Raby, Ben: *100 Things Capitals Fans Should Know & Do Before They Die* (Chicago, Illinois: Triumph Books, 2018).

Wire Services and Newspapers

Associated Press

Canadian Press

Globe & Mail

Ottawa Sun

San Jose Mercury-News

St. Paul Pioneer Press

Winnipeg Free-Press

Winnipeg Sun

Websites

arizonacoyotes.com
buffalosabres.com
carolinahurricanes.com
cbc.ca
dailyfaceoff.com
eliteprospects.com
hockeydb.com
hockey-reference.com
ingoalmag.com
nhl.com
sportsnet.ca
thehockeynews.com
theplayerstribune.com
tsn.ca
vault.si.com